LEARNING TO
SCALE

The secret to growing a fast
and resilient company

LEARNING TO SCALE

The secret to growing a fast and resilient company

Regis Medina
Foreword by Benoît Charles-Lavauzelle

Copyright @ April 2020, Régis Medina
All rights reserved.
ISBN 978-2-9571074-0-7

CONTENTS

~ **Preface** — page 8

1. **Introduction** — page 12

2. **How we limit growth** — page 26

3. **Learning as a Strategy** — page 48

4. **Your Lean Journey** — page 82

5. **The practice** — page 98

   1 FIND TO FACE — page 100

      5.1.1 Start from the gemba — page 102
      5.1.2 Seek to earn customer's smiles — page 118
      5.1.3 Make value flow — page 140
      5.1.4 Stop the line — page 192
      5.1.5 Create basic stability — page 212

   2 FACE TO FRAME — page 236
   3 FRAME TO FORM — page 254
   4 FORM TO FIND — page 270

6. **The Lean Strategy** — page 294

PREFACE

Society is challenging traditional top-down hierarchical companies to be less short-term focused, more people-centric and less dangerous for the planet. In this context it is critical to find new ways of building successful companies. This book describes such a new and revolutionary way. Let's illustrate it through my own experience.

When I finished my studies in 2006, the job opportunities were far less exciting than they are today thanks to the startup boom. Still, I tried. First I did an internship in a strategic consultancy firm and after a few months working more than 70 hours a week, mostly to improve powerpoint presentations and Excel models, I fell ill and realised that my motivation and my resistance were not good enough for this job.

I therefore decided to look elsewhere and give traditional industry a try. I applied for a job with a big industrial company. During our first interaction, I was asked to take a psycho-technical test in an HR agency, and never got to speak to a real person from the company itself. Also, no-one bothered to present the company nor discuss my potential role. I considered the situation totally absurd, and decided to look elsewhere.

In those days, there were no cool startups to work for in France, which would have been a third possibility for me to try. That's why I decided to start my own venture with the idea to create my own job where I could find joy in my work, have an impact and learn every day. When I co-created Theodo in 2009, a software consulting firm, we were lucky enough to quickly find our first customers.

The first months were exciting. We learned the basics of our industry and also some management. Our credibility grew thanks to the accumulation of customer references. We were profitable, which reassured us about the sustainability of the business. However, growth was not where we expected it to be. In 2011, with an annual turnover of eight hundred thousand euros, we decided to give ourselves two years to reach at least 2 million in revenues. At the time, we did not have a clear strategy to get there but we had a lot of ambition because we wanted to live the "startup" experience or nothing.

With faster growth, came the first doubts. A customer at the end of a project offered to pay only half the bill because he was only half satisfied. Another said that, since his understanding of the market had changed during the project, he had to redo everything. Unfortunately, even when the client was satisfied, the project was not always considered a success. For instance, one of our project teams spent three times more than expected, which had catastrophic consequences on the profitability of our young company. Every single problem escalated directly to my business partner and I, and stress started building up. We had a hard time understanding why our teams were making such mistakes.

We finished 2011 completely exhausted. The company growth was not at the expected level and problems were growing much faster than our revenue. We felt stuck and our professional life was at a crossroad. If customers were sometimes frustrated and dissatisfied, our employees also suffered from this situation.

In early 2012, I was lucky to attend a workshop led by a Lean coach on PDCA. I didn't know what Lean or PDCA was at the time, but the talk immediately triggered my interest: according to the speaker, there was a method for solving problems in business! I went to see him at the end of the workshop and invited him a few weeks later to Theodo.

I have been coached by a Lean expert for seven years and my perception of the manager role has radically changed: I have learnt to better define what I expect from employees, to set up a chain of help for everyone in the event of difficulties and to take any opportunity to help them grow instead of asking them to follow rules and orders. I also have learnt to go to the field, i.e. where people work and customers consume our services, before making any strategic decision. The bigger the business, the more difficult and fundamental it gets to stay in touch with reality.

Two years after the great challenge we gave ourselves in 2011, we actually exceeded our initial objective, reaching 3 million euros in turnover. Seven years later, the company has scaled ten times to reach 35 million euros and now has more than 300 employees spread over 4 countries. Without lean, we would not have achieved this. Worse, we would have probably quit with intense exhaustion.

Lean is not only a strategy to succeed your own company, it is also a strategy to tackle two of the most profound challenges humanity has to deal with over the next decades: 1) make work more interesting to engage the new Y generation, and 2) continue our incredible technical and economic growth without exhausting the planet. The Lean strategy is about doing a lot better with a lot less by leveraging people's ingenious ideas, instead of exploiting infinitely limited resources. What is the outcome? Smarter companies, more engaged and satisfied employees and more respect for the environment.

However, lean is not a magic wand. It required me to change everything I believed about business, management and leadership. Without a Sensei to help and some great books to read, It would have been impossible. The good news for those who want to start this journey is that Learning to Scale is an amazing asset to achieve this transformation. This practical book will get you started: it will give you concrete first steps and I believe will help you learn at least twice as fast as I did.

~ *Benoît Charles-Lavauzelle,*
Theodo co-founder

MISCONCEPTIONS

A software development team works on a user interface design for a seemingly unimportant back-office operation. The engineers consider two different approaches and settle on the simplest one because it requires two days of development instead of four.

The team does not realize that this design makes it difficult for back-office agents to operate the service. The operations team is wasting lots of time on each case, and customers start to notice.

A few weeks later, pressure from customers pushes the CEO to add four more people to the back-office team. Four people who spend hours every day on boring and meaningless tasks. Four extra salaries that make profitability harder to reach for the company.

The software development team remains unaware of the problem. Not that they are stupid—the team is composed of smart and committed engineers. They just have no clear feedback on their work, no way to learn how to become better at it.

The fixes requested by the head of back-office operations are now waiting in the product road map, probably for months.

What if the engineers better understood how their product was about to be used before making this mistake?

MISCONCEPTIONS

A sales representative sends a proposal, convinced that she perfectly understands her client needs and is offering a very good technical solution for a fair price.

She does not realize that she spent the last meeting pushing her sales pitch, leaving almost no time for the customer to talk. The customer did not say much, but his decision was already made.

The customer does not want a rigid, one-size-fits-all solution. He is looking for a long-term relationship with a trustworthy business partner. As he is comparing alternatives, he now takes much longer to respond to the various calls of the sales representative.

The sales cycle is long, but the sales representative does not know why. She is wasting time with her proposal and will never really know why the sale failed. She is too busy repeating the same mistake with the next customer to meet her quotas for this quarter.

This misconception has real consequences on her work experience—the constant stress of not meeting quota, of having to wait endlessly for customer answers, of being rejected after intense periods of effort. It also has a direct impact on the profit and loss statement of the business, with revenue goals not met and a larger than needed sales team on the payroll.

What if she learned how to better establish rapport with her leads, understand their expectations perfectly, and craft customized, spot-on proposals? How different would the company trajectory be if the entire sales team did the same?

MISCONCEPTIONS

The executive team of a 100 - person company spends two days off-site, in a beautiful resort, to draft the new strategy and design the new organization for the next quarter.

They name new department heads and set ambitious performance goals, convinced that this will bring clarity and commitment. They prepare a compelling story, a detailed and aggressive deployment road map, and a nice pep talk for the next all-hands meeting. They don't realize that these changes are about to make life harder for half the company, leading to a drop in customer satisfaction and the departure of key employees.

The misconceptions upon which they built the strategy have real consequences on the trajectory of the business—employee morale, ability to attract new talent, reputation among customers, revenue, profit, etc.

1

INTRODUCTION

What if this executive team learned how to engage teams and drive change from the ground up, in a smooth way, rather than shuffling things around again and again in the hope of finding something that works?

1 INTRODUCTION

Rash, uninformed decisions based on misconceptions lead to a colossal waste of talent, time and resources that slows companies down and limits growth.

The lean education system is the antidote.

1
INTRODUCTION

FORGET EVERYTHING YOU KNOW ABOUT LEAN

MANUFACTURING TRICKS

A set of tools to improve processes and building efficient factories

COST CUTTING PROJECTS

Improvement projects led by big consulting firms to get quick results

LEAN STARTUP

Iterate fast with a MVP, pivot your way until you reach product/market fit.

AGILE DEVELOPMENT

Organize the flow of tasks to quickly produce software that meets user needs

The goal of this book is to introduce you to a deeper understanding of lean so that you can build a faster, people- and customer-centric company.

A company that can adapt swiftly to changes in its environment.

1

INTRODUCTION

A GREAT OPPORTUNITY

When you start paying attention to all the mistakes around you, you realize the colossal amount of waste that our companies generate day in and day out: a waste of time, a waste of money, but above all a waste of people's true potential. These mistakes gradually slow our companies down, until they lose the support of their customers and become easy prey for faster, more aggressive competitors.

This phenomenon takes its toll on all society. More than a third of the food we produce is thrown away. A third of the employees worldwide report having experienced some kind of burnout.

This might sound depressing, but it actually represents a great opportunity for you. There is a vast trove of potential waitin to be unlocked—a potential for much better products at lower costs, a potential for better working conditions, a potential for a better use of our planet's resources. What you need is a proven business model to tap into it.

Starting from the mid-1950s, Toyota pioneered a radical new model called the Toyota Production System (TPS). It attracted the attention of business thinkers in the 1980s when the small, nearly bankrupt Japanese company started transforming into a global, powerful competitor. Over the years all manufacturers were gradually forced to adopt its main principles to catch up with its performance.

It later became the basis for impressive business turnarounds, starting with the Wiremold company in the U.S. From 2006 to 2013, it was the framework that Amazon used to build its worldwide operations system. It also inspired the CEO of Pixar on with ideas of how to build an industrial-scale creative organization.

In fact, "lean" refers to the study of the TPS outside of Toyota. But so far lean has been largely misunderstood. In the past 40 years, managers and consultants have framed it as a set of tools to optimize processes and improve operational efficiency. It was still enough to take the industrial world by storm at the end of the last century, with principles such as Just-in-Time or Zero Defects providing the first adopters with a strong competitive advantage.

In the 2000s, it transformed the new economy by changing how digital products were made, first with agile software development methods and more recently with the Lean Startup movement.

However successful, these approaches have only scratched the surface of what lean has to offer.

The Lean Strategy is a proven approach for harnessing the power of good thinking from everyone in the company.
It's the only business strategy based on how people think.

THE BREAKTHROUGH

In 2017, a group of executives and lean experts—Michael Ballé, Daniel Jones, Jacques Chaize, and Orest Fiume—published a groundbreaking book, The Lean Strategy.

After 40 years of research and hands-on practice, the book presents for the first time the concept of lean as a complete business strategy, based on a simple but powerful idea:

> **When people better understand what they do and why, They're better at everything they touch and the company moves faster.**

Companies of all sizes are already demonstrating the incredible results of this strategy. The goal of the companion book that you are reading now is to provide you with the concepts and tools you need to start your own lean journey and reap the benefits of the Lean Strategy for your own company.

HOW WE LIMIT GROWTH

GROWING PAINS

You made it! After months of intense effort, your company has finally taken off. As your reputation spreads across your ecosystem, customer orders start pouring in, so you crank up your hiring efforts to keep up the pace. Your company keeps growing, traction increases, and investors start to take notice. With a fresh influx of cash, you can speed things up further.

Your company is soon starting to exhibit visible signs of success—the large offices, the dozens of people on the company group pictures, the flattering press releases. But this apparent success comes with new challenges. The company grows into a flurry of activity. People are overworked, customer requests pile up, middle managers keep asking for more recruits. As more people join the company, managers find themselves with too many people to handle. With so many newcomers left on their own, you see mistakes and defects proliferate, and everything seems to take longer than before.

When market conditions change and you need to change direction fast to seize new opportunities you find the company too slow to adapt.

For the executive team, this translates into constant pressure to intervene to fix dozens of thorny issues a day just to keep the business afloat. This works for a time, and even feels exhilarating…until you feel exhausted and cannot take it any longer.

And as you see people making mistake after mistake, the natural reaction is to crave more control.

The new credo becomes "industrialization." You manage to convince experienced managers from larger, more mature companies to join you to clarify roles, improve processes, and set up robust reporting systems.

But as the company matures, you eventually realize that everything seems to take even longer. Customer satisfaction keeps declining. Key employees decide to quit. Morale plummets. Costs rise faster than expected. Sales figures start to disappoint.

Now what you wish for is your company becoming more agile, like in its early days.

This scenario is a well-known phenomenon, one of the core "first principles" of business. It even deserves its own immutable law.

BALLÉ'S IRON LAW OF SCALE-UP

With fast growth, silo and complexity costs increase faster than revenue

This phenomenon is called the "big company disease."

The first symptoms appear in the first years of any company:

— Defending **process** over **customers**

— Defending **silos** over **teamwork**

— Rewarding **compliance** over **initiative**

— Confusing **legacy** and **heritage technologies**

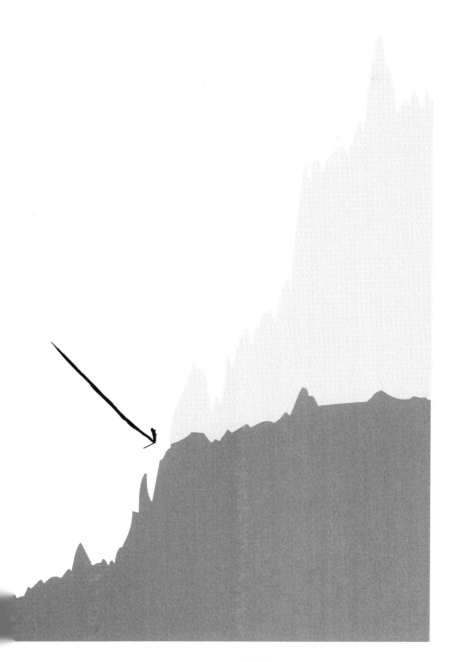

2
HOW WE LIMIT GROWTH

DEFENDING PROCESS OVER CUSTOMERS

The partners of a venture capital firm are reflecting on a recent series of missed opportunities. They are considering different strategies, ranging from changing their financing terms to improving the brand.

What they don't realize is that as they have grown in size, they have evolved a rigid and lengthy process for filtering investment opportunities. Junior analysts follow the script they have been taught, filling up detailed reports for the senior partners.

From the perspective of the entrepreneur, dealing with the firm is an excruciating series of meetings spent repeating the same pitch to many people, with months wasted without being able to work properly on the growth of their company.

2
HOW WE LIMIT GROWTH

Following the process designed by the senior partners has become more important than serving promising entrepreneurs.

What would be the trajectory of this firm if the investment team learned how to work together to produce term sheets in a matter of days, or even hours?

DEFENDING SILOS OVER TEAMWORK

The weekly executive meeting is tense, as usual.

The VP of sales is lashing at the chief operating officer, complaining about the fact that customer projects are always late and major incidents are on the rise. This hurts the reputation of the company and makes it difficult for the sales team to meet its quotas for the quarter. The VP of sales is questioning whether, given the chaos in the operations teams, the COO is the right person to lead the activity. The COO, in turn, is mad at the VP of sales because contracts are signed without her approval, with deadlines and cost targets that are impossible for her to meet with the resources available.

The situation is dire enough that top members of both the sales and operations teams are quitting, but the two executives cannot find a way to work together.

A similar dynamic is at play between the chief marketing officer and the chief technology officer. The CMO complains that she cannot reduce her acquisition costs without important data that should be sent by the tech team. This request has been on the road map for ages and is frequently postponed. The CTO is challenging her on the fact that the specifications she sent are unusable and that the last two reports she requested have never been used.

For these executives, reaching department-level goals has become more important than helping each other for the benefit of the company.

REWARDING COMPLIANCE OVER INITIATIVE

A young and energetic software engineer recently joined the company.

In the first weeks, she noticed that parts of the system could be improved in just a few hours, saving time for all of the 10-people team on most future-user interface developments. She is surprised when her team leader dismisses her proposal with no convincing explanation.

A few months and a half-dozen similar episodes later, she notices another possible major improvement to the system. This time she prefers to remain silent and stick to the tasks that were given to her.

In the same period, one of the product managers has been hard at work studying user needs and behavior, leading many customer interviews. When he hears the VP of product dismiss his idea, he realizes that in the past year not a single one of his suggestions has been implemented. From his perspective, the situation is clear: he is not paid to improve the product and satisfy customers, he is paid for doing the grunt work needed to implement the brilliant ideas of his bosses. He is stuck with a dilemma: should he stay and do the minimum required, enjoying more free time and the company's perks, or should he quit to find a place where he can contribute his ideas?

In both cases, middle management is unwittingly dampening initiative by enforcing compliance. This leads the high-potential talent leaving the company; the ones who stay are people who follow the rules without asking too many questions.

CONFUSING LEGACY AND HERITAGE TECHNOLOGIES

In the mid-2000s, a software editor was selling a personal finance application based on a then-popular technology. It was a desktop application, installed on the user's computer.

A few web-based competitors started entering the market. Within the company, engineers were defending the desktop technology over the web-based one with sound arguments:

— The desktop app was much faster.

— It allowed for more advanced interactions, providing a better user experience.

— Customers were reluctant to let a web company host their financial statements and preferred to keep them on their own computers.

— Engineers had developed a deep knowledge of desktop technology, and they had built many custom-designed tools that made them highly productive.

— Turning to a web-based application would require a near-complete, and thus very expensive, rewrite of the whole product.

There was never a specific moment when their application became obsolete. But year after year, the web technologies were getting better, customers were getting accustomed to trusting their personal data with internet companies, and the software editor's codebase was becoming larger and larger, making the switch even more expensive.

This company is now defunct. Many companies take off by exploiting the advantage of new technology over existing incumbents on the market. It's always better to be on the right side of disruption, but becoming the one being disrupted comes earlier than we think. And it starts with confusing legacy and heritage technologies.

2 HOW WE LIMIT GROWTH

The engineering team considered for too long that their desktop technology was a heritage technology—a competitive advantage—when in reality it had become a legacy technology - a hindrance.

CORE ASSUMPTIONS

The symptoms of the big company disease are the consequences of the current approach to scaling companies, which is directly based on the business theories pioneered in the early 20th century by people such as Frederic Winston Taylor, Henri Ford, and Alfred Sloan.
Even in modern, internet-era companies, the fundamental model is not different from what Charlie Chaplin depicted in his 1936 movie Modern Times.

We now take all these elements for granted:

— **Proposing the same service or product to a large panel of customers is the key to profitability.** But as competition increases customers are faced with a large choice, and a one-size-fits-all approach becomes a liability.

— **Decomposing activities into small, repeatable actions helps increase quality and productivity.** People however quickly learn to follow the script and forget why the motions were designed this way. As soon as the context changes, they don't know how to adapt properly.

— **Specializing roles allows everyone to keep focused on their tasks.** But after a while, every department loses touch with the needs of the others—or those of end customers—and starts competing against them for resources.

— **Interchangeable people make it possible for the company to operate even in the face of high turnover.** The downside is that you cannot take the risk to invest in developing star employees, but what happens when a competitor does?

— **Centralized control is needed to coordinate actions across the entire company.** But as the company grows, the corporate team loses touch with the reality of day-to-day operations.

— **Reporting systems are needed to give executives a vision of how things are going on in the teams.** But it is not long before people start feeding them the information they want to hear: "Everything's okay!"

— **Automation is the best response to productivity issues.** Except when productivity could be doubled or tripled in a matter of days if people learned to work better together.

Note that there is nothing inherently bad about these ideas, and a lean company will probably use all of them to some extent. What we need to understand though, is that the way these principles are used in practice has unexpected consequences. They limit people's initiative and personal development. They create factions within the company. They make change difficult. But perhaps the most dangerous consequence of these ideas is the way executives usually craft the strategy of the company.

STRATEGY IN A WORLD OF COMMAND & CONTROL

DEFINE ⟶

The management team defines the high-level challenges of the company in a boardroom or during an offsite, based in part on inputs from investors and other CEOs, and in part on their own interpretation of where the business is going.

DECIDE ⟶

They weigh the pros and cons of a couple of alternatives, discuss scenarios at length, and end up deciding on the best course of action. The plan becomes the new strategy of the company.

4D

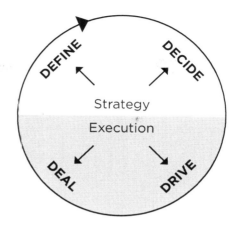

DRIVE ⟶ **DEAL**

The management team crafts a compelling story to sell the strategy to investors and employees. They create a comprehensive roadmap, name people in charge of the major milestones, set ambitious performance goals, and start driving the strategy across all departments.

After a few weeks the teams struggle with the new plan. Managers are stuck dealing with the real-world damage of a decision that was taken far from the reality of the field. As they struggle with operational problems, they start thinking that a change in strategy is much needed... and the cycle starts again.

CONSEQUENCES OF 4D THINKING

Building the strategy far from the reality of operations, based on misconceptions, leads to major sources of waste in:

MORALE

On a day-to-day basis, employees want to get their job done with the less hassle. Every 4D cycle brings unwanted changes and problems that prevent them from doing a good job, proving time and again that their managers are completely out of touch with the reality of their work.

TALENT

The most talented employees and managers are assigned to the new plan. At first they just resent being handed a strategy from the higher-ups, but when the plan starts falling apart and they feel unable to make it work, it slowly develops into full-blown burnout.

INNOVATION

Innovation is crippled because the company only benefits from the ideas of a handful of people, and often people whose hands-on experience with technology and deep relations with customers are more a distant memory than a current reality.

REVENUE

The ideas cascaded in 4D mode rarely result in real hits from a customer perspective. These missed opportunities can be very costly, forcing the owners to look for new investment more often than they would like to.

PROFIT

Developing products that won't sell or solve any real problems, disrupting the daily operations of the company all contribute to wasting a significant portion of hard-earned profits. And that's without counting the gains that could be obtained if managers took more time to take care of their teams.

AN ALTERNATIVE: THE LEAN EDUCATION SYSTEM

Even though the drawbacks of Command & Control are well known, it remains the most common management framework because it stems from a natural human reaction: the need for control.

To fight its perverse effects, executives, managers, and researchers have been looking for different approaches, ranging from building sophisticated reward mechanisms to giving people complete autonomy. Companies have been experimenting with radical new models such as the liberated enterprise, or holacracy.

But in all these cases, the discussion remains in the realm of control: who owns it, and how much to exert it. Lean takes a completely different approach. It is a complete business strategy based on how people can better learn on the job.

**Lean is not about
how we organize work,
it's about how we think about it.**

**It's not a production system,
it's an education system.**

LEARNING
AS A STRATEGY

THE BREAKTHROUGH

The Lean Strategy is a unique and proven model for scaling strong and healthy companies.
It is an alternative to the 4D approach, based on a simple premise:

Creating more and more value for each customer to foster trust and loyalty

by engaging everyone, every day, to improve something in their work to better think and learn about what they do

leads to a sustainable growth that improves the lives of customers, employees and shareholders, and helps build a better society.

The Lean Strategy is a complete system for turning this vision into reality.

3
LEARNING AS A STRATEGY

BECOMING A LEARNING ORGANIZATION

Placing learning at the center of the strategy is not just a matter of company slogans and wishful thinking. It's about developing two specific know-hows:

Actively looking for what we don't know that limits our performance

Actively developing the knowledge and skills of everyone

3
LEARNING AS A STRATEGY

LEARNING ON THE JOB (1/2)

The new VP of engineering is under pressure from the executive team to deliver an ambitious update to the company's flagship product. Given the short timeframe, he knows from past experience that adding more engineers will not help much because the new hires will take months before making a significant contribution, and in the meantime they will require lots of attention from the senior, most productive engineers.

As a lean practitioner, he also knows that there must be a large potential for improvement in the current practices of the engineering department, and this potential lies in the misconceptions of product managers and engineers. But how to uncover them?

He always starts with quality issues, but in this case it is all the more important because customer satisfaction is low due to poor product quality, and roughly a third of development efforts go into bug fixes.

He thus spends some time with an engineer and a product manager to study the last fixed defects. Rather than looking at statistics, they take specific examples and dive deep to get to their root causes.

3

LEARNING AS A STRATEGY

He is actively trying to uncover what are the things that the team ignores that lead to these quality issues

LEARNING ON THE JOB (2/2)

Two main insights soon emerge. First, some members of the product management team write specifications without considering all edge cases. Given the large volume of customers, all these this-should-never-happen situations end up happening. Second, developers lack a clear understanding on how to design robust code. They make unsafe assumptions on the parameters they receive or the functions they call in their code.

He starts by engaging the product department in reducing the number of bugs, mainly for the sake of doing work the teams can be proud of.

He then shows the head of product how to review specifications with his product managers in one-on-one sessions, to teach them how to better analyze a situation and consider edge cases. He then sets up a way for developers to report abnormalities in specifications so that product managers can have continuous feedback on their work.

He also works with tech leads to clarify their theory of what makes code robust, building on their experience, but also reviewing classic books and articles on the topic. Tech leads use this knowledge to train engineers within the existing code review process. They soon discover large areas of the product that can be fixed to improve robustness for a reasonable effort.

In just a few weeks, the number of weekly defects is halved and the team is in a much better position to reach its goals.

3
LEARNING AS A STRATEGY

He creates an environment where the daily work conducts to the rapid acquisition of knowledge and skills.

HOW WE LEARN

If learning is paramount, then the first thing we need to learn about is... learning. How do adults learn?
To start with, there is one golden rule of learning:

Rule #1 :
People learn when they want to learn

This golden rule has four corollaries:

We tend to learn more about what we already know and like, and avoid topics we like less.
However, the business context of the company requires us to develop specific skills which may not be those we want to learn. For instance, a developer is excited to learn about new technologies when the business would rather benefit from him learning how to write code without bugs.
To create a good learning environment, you are therefore faced with two questions: how do you find what skills to develop, and how can you bring people to learn them?

We want to see how the learning helps us, and put it in practice immediately.
This means that you need to keep the learning very close—both in terms of topic and in time—to the use of the new skills.

We need autonomy to try things on our own.
This supposes that we are not forced to follow a rigid script, and that we have constant feedback on the consequences of our actions.

We want to feel safe.
We need to practice these new skills in a low-risk, friendly environment.

This has practical implications on how to manage learning at work.

MANAGING TO LEARN

Using learning as a strategy requires a fundamentally different management approach than the traditional Command & Control.

Command & Control

	Give directions on the actions to be performed	Make sure that actions are executed according to plan
Impacts on learning	Deprives people of an understanding of why things are done this way, as well as the ability to try different things on their own.	
Underlying assumptions	«Since people don't know what to do, we need to give them clear instructions on what to do and how, and then set up mechanisms to know when they deviate from the plan in order to put them back on track.»	

Orient & Support

| Clarify the compelling outcomes to achieve | Help people speak up and clarify the method they use to reach the goal |

Fosters total voluntary participation in learning and self-improvement across the company.

«We hired smart and committed people. If we are all clear on our common goals, we can let them contribute and then develop the skills and knowledge they need to overcome obstacles as they come.»

TWO MANAGEMENT APPROACHES

Command & Control

«Sales figures are disappointing. Everyone is working in a different way, so I have revised the sales pitch, designed a new sales process, and created a new proposal template that you just need to fill out to save time.

I have also raised the variable part of your compensation so that you are all fully motivated.

I will set weekly appointments with each of you, starting in the next few days, to answer your questions and help you implement this new process successfully.»

Orient & Support

«We are behind target on our sales figures, so we need to better understand what's going on. As you all know, all the problems the customer faces in purchasing our products translate into a longer sales cycle. I have updated our sales boards so that each sales rep can better see how long they have been chasing each prospect.
Starting tomorrow, I will come and study a few cases with you daily in short, one-on-one sessions, so that we can dig into specific cases and learn what prevents individual customers from buying from us, and how you can find better ways to establish rapport with them and help them.»

LEARNING STARTS FROM THE TOP

As an executive, it is very tempting to read all the above thinking about how other people should better learn in your company. And to an extent, the Lean Strategy does require having everyone learning on the job, every day.

However, remaining at this level does not usually last long. As people learn and uncover new ways to work and to think, they soon realize that top management is still fixated on its own beliefs. When new proposals keep being rejected by the higher-ups, they wonder why they should be the ones being open minded while their leaders fail to walk the talk.

There is a deeper reason for not limiting learning to everyone else: top managers suffer from misconceptions as much as everybody else. The only difference is that when they drive the strategy based on misconceptions, they inflict more damage to the company.

What the lean community has learned over the decades is that putting learning at the center of the strategy starts from the top. In other words:

The Lean Strategy can only succeed when fully embraced by the CEO and the executive team.

But what if you are not the CEO? Do not despair; you can still learn and get results in your own team or department, but don't expect a global turnaround of the company. Transforming the company requires a commitment from the CEO, and a very different approach to strategy than the 4D cycle.

STRATEGY IN A WORLD OF CONTINUOUS LEARNING

FIND ⟶   FACE ⟶

The CEO and the management team go frequently on the field to help teams solve specific types of day-to-day problems.

They face the main issues of the business, starting with their own misconceptions, and take a '"helicopter view" to find the challenges that limit growth and could change the company trajectory.

4F

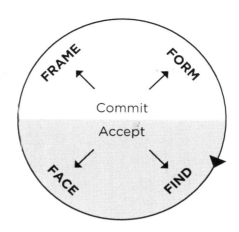

FRAME  **FORM**

They cascade these high-level challenges throughout the company, framing them in such a way that every team can contribute to the global learning effort.

The management team supports the teams in finding innovative ways to solve the company's challenges and to design and deliver better products, to sustain growth and stay relevant over time.

STOP DISRUPTING THE BUSINESS

Adopting a 4F approach to strategy implies a first commitment for the executive: stop hurting the company! This means taking a hard look at typical 4D activities:

— **Re-organizing departments**
— **Pushing new product ideas**
— **Deploying new processes, workflows, and tools**
— **Outsourcing** new parts of the activity

Sure, being able to enact sweeping changes like these feels empowering, if not addictive, until you realize it often amounts to playing the sorcerer's apprentice.

That is probably what makes lean difficult to accept for many managers. It comes down to a trade-off:

Command & Control		Orient & Support
"I lead a company that I have built as I wanted, and that I can change it at will, but my people are always lagging behind."		"I lead a company that is nimble and can adapt quickly to new situations… but I avoid implementing major changes on a whim."

But if shuffling things around is out of the manager's playbook, what is left?

These activities still exist in lean companies. They are just led in a very different way, which should become clearer as you learn about the whole strategy.

Where do you start? Making sure things actually work.

A STRATEGY OF BUSINESS CONTINUITY

At its core, the lean strategy is focused on business continuity: delivering a steady flow of value to customers over time, without interruption. This comes from the realization that every incident, every delivery interruption, every angry customer, every employee departure, every strike, every restructuring erodes revenue and profitability.

Business continuity is also an important driver for a higher valuation, since the price of the company reflects the trust of investors in its future. A predictable and constantly improving business is a great source of confidence.

Business continuity is far from stagnation. It is a dynamic state, which needs everyone in the company constantly reacting to external challenges—from small, daily hiccups to large-scale changes in the company's environment. It is a strategy of extreme adaptation.

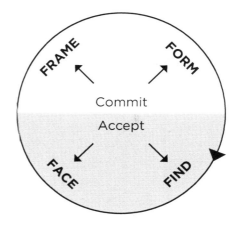

For this reason, the lean executive always starts with Find: understanding deeply what factors disrupt business continuity, before taking a step back to reflect on where to take the next step at a strategic level - a move called the helicopter.

THE HELICOPTER WORKOUT

For the CEO or the executive, practicing the 4F cycle helps develop the ability to start from local details, zoom out at a high-level strategic level, and zoom in again.

It is about developing the ability to hold the reality of the whole business in one's head. It is an alternative to becoming a single-mode leader: the high-level dreamer unable to understand what's going on for real, or the day-to-day firefighter unable to step back.

It is also about developing the ability, as a leader, to keep engaging people on a personal level even as the business grows.

This frequent back-and-forth between the daily activity and the high level view helps the executive constantly drive the adaptation of the company in a changing environment.

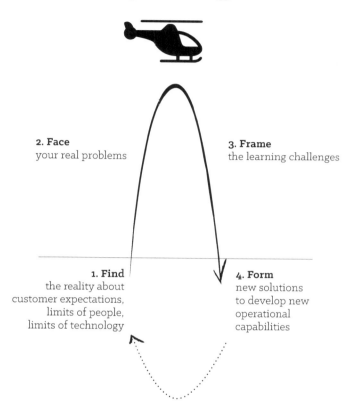

A MENTAL MODEL TO DRIVE LEARNING

In practice, maintaining business continuity means helping the teams tackle the myriad problems that arise every day. But for maximum impact, you need to know what problems are worth solving first, and how to solve them the right way. In other words, you need a robust mental model for what constitutes a good improvement.

The TPS is such a model.

The Toyota Production System was formulated internally over decades by Toyota to train its managers. Eventually, a few Toyota veterans started using a new name, the Thinking People System, because it better conveyed its intention.

The TPS is a powerful guide for making people think deeper to improve any kind of business operation. It has proven robust across industries, for all company sizes. The same model is used for thinking about how to recruit faster, how to develop sales, how to improve quality in production, how to improve morale across the company, and how to find a competitive positioning in an industry.

The TPS is a comprehensive mental model for experienced managers. It can be described in an hour, but it never ceases to reveal new insights after years of practice.

```
                    Customer Satisfaction
              Value Analysis / Value Engineering
   Safely    Quality    Lead-Time    Cost    Energy performance
```

	Just in Time		Jidoka	
	Takt Time		Andon	
	Continuous one-pièce flow		Poka yoke	
	Pull system		Human/ machine separation	

Heijunka	Standard work	Kaizen
5S	Problem Solving	TPM

The TPS - Thinking People System

A PROVEN BLUEPRINT FOR SUSTAINED GROWTH

As a first approximation, the TPS highlights the main components of a sustainable growth strategy:

Just in Time

Reduce the lead time of operations by surfacing and addressing stagnation issues

Stability

Create the conditions for everyone to contribute improvement ideas and learn on the job

Customer satisfaction

Develop loyal customers
by catering to their individual needs

Reinvest improvement gains
into a steady flow of new products

Jidoka

Perform operations right the first
time by stopping at every defect
to remove its cause

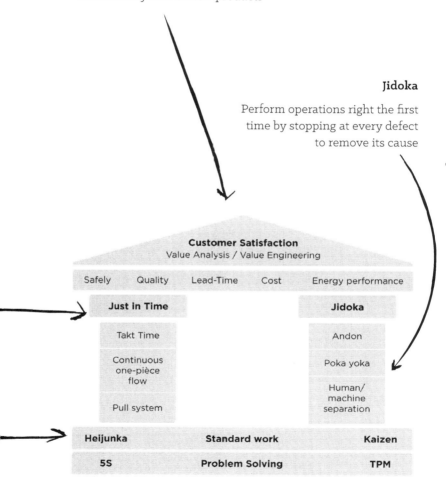

A SET OF LEARNING EXERCISES TO DRIVE GROWTH

By considering the TPS as an ideal situation, we can step back and study our business to find improvement insights. This leads to five main questions, presented in greater detail later in this book.

Just in Time

What prevents us from having a steady, continuous flow of value across the company, without stagnation?

Stability

In what ways do we prevent team members from working in the conditions needed for them to contribute their ideas for improvement?

Customer satisfaction

Do we deeply understand the situation
and needs of each individual customer?
How could we create more value?

What do we need to change in the next evolution
of our product to create more value for our customers?

Jidoka

What is preventing team
members from doing quality
work right first time?
Do local leaders help them as
much as they should?

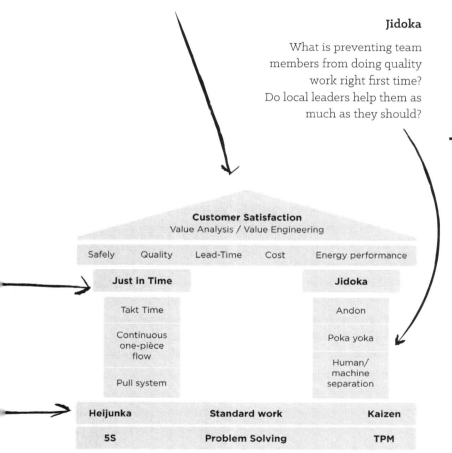

LEARNING THE TPS

Getting familiar with the TPS is a prerequisite for reaping the benefits of the lean strategy.

The bar is admittedly quite high—there are lots of concepts to master, and most of them are counterintuitive. It will take months, if not years, to become familiar with this way of thinking. This should be no surprise since lean embodies the expert knowledge of management. It covers many of the questions that a manager faces:

— How do we improve performance for customers without putting too much pressure on the teams?
— How do we industrialize operations in a way that does not inhibit creativity?
— How do we adapt to changing business conditions and keep relevant and profitable over time?
— How do we attract and retain talent?
— How do we best combine automation and human work?
— How do we align teams and departments?
— etc.

You can consider lean and the TPS as a 20-year shortcut in your own career as a manager.

This is worth some form of investment! How do you start?

YOUR
LEAN JOURNEY

HOW TO FAIL AT LEAN

Let's start with the easy part: failing. Failing at lean is quite easy, and a path that is well trodden. Here are a few proven tactics to save time and fail even faster.

——— **1. Delegate lean to someone else.** This is the best one. Find someone down the ladder, or a consultant, who has time for all this stuff, and ask for monthly reports to see how the lean initiative is going.

——— **2. Read about lean and watch a few videos until you "get it."** The lean experts and CEOs hone their lean skills through years of deliberate and continuous practice, and they keep repeating that lean is just that: a practice. That is probably because they are a bunch of fanatics. You have no time for this, so just read a few books to grasp the main concepts and that should be enough! (Hmm, how would that fare for tennis?)

——— **3. Inflict lean on other people.** It will soon be obvious for you that lean does not apply in your personal situation: your activities are so varied, you only deal with intellectual and non-repetitive tasks, and so on. Other people in all kinds of business and activities have managed to learn from lean, but they must be facing more favorable conditions than yours. It's much better to challenge all your colleagues with the lean questions, to show them how misguided they are and help them learn. After all their job is much simpler than yours!

────── **4. Put all the lean tools in place, and make sure that people follow them every day.** These tools are necessarily good, so the more you have in place, the better. The most advanced lean CEOs use only a few tools to focus on people development and business growth, but they must be missing lots of potential improvements. So collect as many tools as possible, implement them all, and set up a solid reporting system to ensure they are used by the teams despite their well-known resistance to change. Congratulations, you just replaced an old malfunctioning bureaucracy with a new malfunctioning one!

With all this tongue-in-cheek advice in the open, it's time for an inconvenient truth.

A PERSONAL CHALLENGE

It's not about how you impose lean on other people.

To transform your organization, first transform yourself

4

YOUR LEAN JOURNEY

A PERSONAL PRACTICE

Lean is a practice, much like piano, tennis, karate, or math. It is a practice of improvement.

Like any practice, it comes with its own principles, techniques, and lingo. We practice by improving business situations, by helping other people improve, and we get better at it over time. There are beginners, pros, students, and teachers. There are people practicing at the level of a team, others at the level of a department, others at the level of a whole company, and others yet learning how to accelerate the growth of large, multinational corporations.

How do you learn lean? Just think about how you would approach learning tennis, for instance.

After watching a few people play you start with a few, simple exercises. The first tries are not pretty, but you keep at it and get a few successes. After a while, you hit a plateau, so you read a few books, watch educational videos, and keep practicing until you make progress again. Step-by-step you learn the vocabulary, the techniques. You meet other practitioners and look for the masters to emulate.

As you feel more competent, you hit another plateau. You are now committed to the sport, so you find an instructor and take lessons to learn even faster.

After a few months, you start noticing a clear difference with untrained people. After a few years and some impressive results under your belt, you find yourself unable to explain in detail how you do it. You see, feel, and do things in a different way, but you cannot explain it—you can just show them how to start their own journey, following the same path that you did.

It is exactly the same for lean.

What this means in practice is that you should not overthink things before trying them out. Lean is more of a "do first, understand later" approach. To learn fast, just commit to doing the exercises presented in this book. Get comfortable trying things out, doing it poorly at first, reflecting a bit, and trying again

~~Understand › Prepare › Try~~

Try › See › Understand

ENGAGE EVERYBODY ONE BY ONE

How do you engage the whole company? The usual Command & Control approach would consist of announcing a company-wide lean transformation, bringing in consultants, and creating a plan to train and involve all the teams in using the lean tools. In practice, such an approach will probably fizzle out. It takes time and personal attention for one individual to get on board and be willing to learn. Spreading the effort to everybody at once will probably result in too little support given to those who want to learn, and too much pressure on those who are not yet ready.

Lean is not something that you put in place across the company in a matter of weeks. It is more akin to a series of exercises that you perform to get a deeper and broader understanding of your situation. Once you get familiar with these exercises you can help other people in your organization do the same.

A more robust approach thus involves going into the field and trying to practice the lean concepts described in this book. You will soon find people who are eager to learn with you. You can then spend more time with them, support them, and get the first successes with them in a positive atmosphere. Over time others will join, and the few who resist the strong emphasis put on learning and self-improvement will eventually find better work opportunities elsewhere.

Even after a few years, do not be surprised to find people with vastly different levels of mastery and motivation about lean in your company. This is a practice; every one learns at their own pace.

WORKING WITH A SENSEI

After the first experience with the tools and principles presented in this book, you will probably want to get a step further. As for any practice, you will learn faster with an instructor. In lean such people are called sensei, much like in the Japanese martial arts tradition.

A sensei is someone who has walked the path before, someone with a deep experience of the TPS in a large variety of business situations.

A sensei is different from a traditional consultant in that she does not bring solutions to you, nor implement solutions for you, because in the end lean is about people taking responsibility for their own learning. This leads to a very specific—and often disorienting—kind of interaction.

A good sensei will bring you into the field, show improvement potential everywhere, bring insights in how to approach it, propose exercises, and challenge you to learn and change. The learning is then for you to embark on.

There are no known repositories or agencies to find a good sensei; you will have to find one by yourself. To separate the grain from the chaff, you can judge the success of executives who worked with them, and check their credentials: most good sensei will be able to trace their lineage back to the Toyota masters of old.

4
YOUR LEAN JOURNEY

HOW TO LEARN WITH THIS BOOK

The Lean Strategy is a system of interdependent concepts and practices. You will find that there is a lot of material to discover - remember, this is about learning how to grow companies!

The material in this book is organized along the 4 phases of the 4F cycle. You can read everything sequentially, or skip parts and discover the system in a different order depending on your current needs.

This book is designed as a reference manual. You will need to get back to it, study and practice its different components, to get familiar with the whole approach and change your thinking.

FIND
Page 100

Craft the strategy from the ground up
How do you engage people in improving the company by solving operational problems day in and day out, while developing their skills and their ability to work together? This section, by far the largest in the book, describes all the elements of the TPS.

FACE
Page 236

Grasp and cherish your real problems
How do you uncover the main challenges of the company and unlock growth? This means facing your own responsibility in these challenges, and helping the executive team to agree on tackling them together.

FRAME
Page 254

Align the whole company around compelling learning goals
How do you align the whole company on a small set of challenges, so that everybody can contribute ideas and grow in line with the common goal?

FORM
Page 270

Innovate every day to stay relevant over time
How do you foster the creativity of everyone in the company to develop new capabilities and adapt to market changes over the years?

LEARNING BY DOING

In each section you will find a series of Time to Practice pages which propose hands-on exercises.

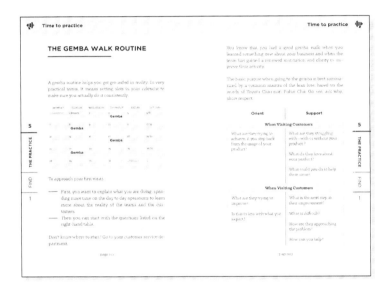

Remember: lean is a practice. Doing these exercises to explore the concepts with your own context is the only way to get deep insights and reap the benefits of this strategy.

4

YOUR LEAN JOURNEY

THE PRACTICE

FIND TO FACE

FIND

Craft the strategy from the ground up

1 START FROM THE GEMBA

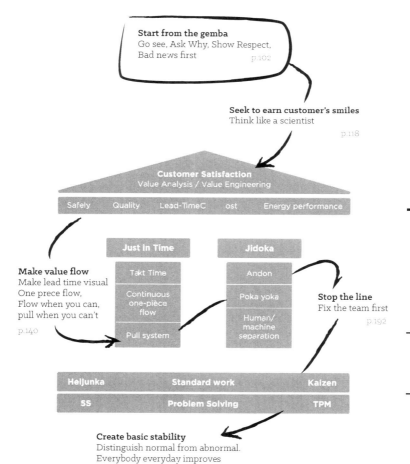

START FROM THE GEMBA

The first commitment of the lean practitioner is to «go to the gemba». Gemba is a Japanese term that means «the place where real things happen."

Depending on your activity and the context, the gemba might be:

—— The shop or the website where customers buy your products
—— The place where customers use your products
—— The office where your teams work
—— The codebase in which your engineers build the features of your product
—— Your suppliers' offices or factories, etc.

Going to the gemba means getting out of your office and visiting either your customers, the people who create value for your customers, or those who support them.

Going to the gemba is no mere tourism, it is a learning expedition. You go there with the intention to learn something.

5

THE PRACTICE

FIND 1

🔊 **Time to practice**

THE GEMBA WALK ROUTINE

A gemba routine helps you get grounded in reality. In very practical terms, it means setting slots in your calendar to make sure you actually do it consistently.

MONDAY	TUESDAY	WEDNESDAY	THURSDAY	FRIDAY	SAT/SUN
31 December	1 January	2	3 **Gemba**	4	5/6
7	8 **Gemba**	9	10	11	12/13
14	15	16	17 **Gemba**	18	19/20
21	22 **Gemba**	23	24	25	26/27
28	29	30	31	1 February	2

To approach your first visits :

—— First, you want to explain what you are doing: spending more time on the day to day operations to learn more about the reality of the teams and the customers.
—— Then you can start with the questions listed on the right-hand table.

Don't know where to start? Go to your customer service department.

Time to practice

You know that you had a good gemba walk when you learned something new about your business and when the team has gained a renewed motivation and clarity to improve their activity.

Orient	Support
When Visiting Customers	
What are they trying to achieve, if you step back from the usage of your product?	What are they struggling with—with or without your product?
	What do they love about your product?
	What could you do to help them more?
When Visiting Teams	
What are they trying to improve?	What is the next step in their improvement?
Is this in line with what you expect?	What is difficult?
	How are they approaching the problem?
	How can you help?

The basic posture when going to the gemba is best summarized by a common mantra of the lean lore, based on the words of Toyota Chairman Fukui Cho: Go see, ask why, show respect.

GO & SEE

Just talking with people will usually not take you far for a simple reason: it keeps the discussion in the realm of opinions. The lean perspective is that current performance is limited by opinions founded on misconceptions, so the potential for improvement lies in rooting out these misconceptions. The best way to do that is by confronting opinions with facts.

You thus want to spend most of your gemba walks looking at things. For instance:

Context	Blah, Blah, Blah
Customer Support	"How are the stats?"
Software Development	"Can you tell me what happened during the last incident?"
Sales	"What should you have done to win this customer?"
Marketing	"Tell me why we ended up sending the newsletter to the wrong people?"

There is reason why Michael and Freddy Ballé's first award-winning lean book was titled «The Gold Mine». There is a vast trove of improvement hidden in the day to day details of work, in the difference between what we think and how things are in reality. As CEOs have found before, you could for instance realize that the expensive rewrite of your product is unnecessary and could be replaced with a few targeted fixes worth a few days of work. Or that lowering prices could be avoided if sales representatives learned how to better create rapport with their customers. Or that the large system or the large factory you wanted to build is not really needed.

Go & See

"Can we look at the last 10 closed tickets?"

"Can we have a look at the code to see where the program failed? And the spec? And the test cases?

"Can you show me the emails and the proposal? "

"Can you show me how the last newsletters was sent?"

ASK "WHY?"

During your gemba walks you will invariably stumble upon unexpected things: people not focussed on what you expected, work not being done the way you thought, problems not being addressed as you would like. You will then be tempted to revert to the Command & Control script: issuing instructions on how to fix the issue. While this might improve things in the short term, it will prevent you from learning what actually caused the situation and it will prevent your people from using their own judgement.

The basic posture of a gemba walk is curiosity: why are things this way? Exploring the reasons behind the actions will lead you to learning something—and if done well, you will quite often be the one changing your mind.

5
THE PRACTICE
FIND
1

SHOW RESPECT

Showing respect to customers, employees and suppliers is a prerequisite for them being engaged with your business. It obviously applies to your own behaviour during the interactions with people, but also to what you pay attention to.

A gemba walk is an exercise in **awareness**. You are looking for signs that the company itself is lacking respect for them, be it by overwork, unnecessary variation, or a difficult working environment. You are also looking for signs of the Big Company Disease. Are people following processes rather than attending customer needs? Are they fighting for their interests at the expense of other teams? Are they oppressed by middle management? Are they defending legacy technology or abandoning heritage technology?

One step further, what does your company look like through their eyes?

5

THE PRACTICE

FIND

1

BAD NEWS FIRST

One consequence of developing a learning mindset and trying to understand what disrupts business continuity is that you become more and more interested in what does not work as expected. Problems, defined as a gap between what we expect and current reality, become your base material for improvement ideas. You want to make them visible and face them to uncover what they have to reveal. You look for them during your gemba walks.

The trouble is, problems make people uncomfortable because they are associated with guilt. No one likes making mistakes and then discussing them with their boss in front of everybody else.

It is not easy to get around this, but you still have a large influence on people depending on the way you react. There is a trade-off: if you are too harsh people will tend to hide problems, and if you are too permissive they risk becoming careless.

A proven approach is the following:

— React to problems with curiosity, thanking people for pointing them out.
— Be less permissive of people making the same mistake twice.

With this approach, you can work towards creating a "bad news first" culture which still remains safe and healthy, and you can face problems heads-on.

SOLVING THE RIGHT PROBLEMS

Going to the gemba is the opportunity for you to engage your teams in solving the right problems. But what problems should you address first?

This is where you use the TPS. It describes four main families of problems to tackle on a daily basis:

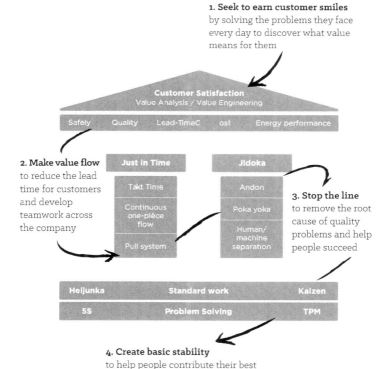

FIND

Craft the strategy from the ground up

2 SEEK TO EARN CUSTOMER'S SMILES

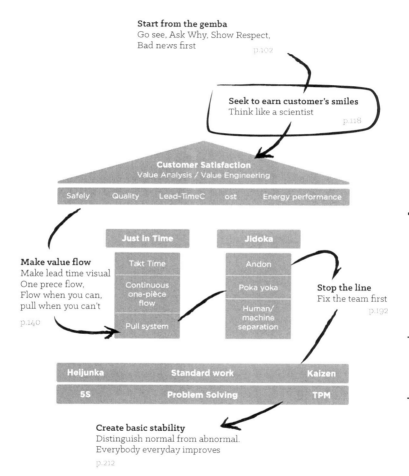

SEEK TO EARN CUSTOMER'S SMILES

Lean is a customer-centric growth strategy. Its basic premise is that if you keep on creating ever more value for customers, and if they stay with you over time, growth will follow. For this reason, the ultimate target of Orient & Support is always the customer.

Current business thinking leads us to think about customers in terms of segments or personas. The trap here is to think in terms of abstractions. In the space you leave between your generic approach and the needs of a specific customer lies an opportunity for a competitor to step in. Conversely, digging deep into the expectations of each customer will uncover opportunities to create more value and accelerate growth.

A lean approach consists in considering every customer as an individual, with her own specific needs and preferences. The ultimate goal is to deeply understand what value means in her eyes. This is a first step before developing the flexibility of the company, i.e. its ability to serve many different customer needs efficiently.

Value always remains elusive, because it means different things to different people, because we don't even know what we really want, and because context, preferences and alternatives are always changing.

To better understand value from the customer perspective, we try to discover:

- **What is he trying to achieve?**
- **How?**
- **What obstacles is he facing?**
- **What alternatives is he considering for getting past these obstacles?**
- **What implicit or explicit criteria does he use to choose one alternative over another?**

The best place to start this exploration is your customer service department, listening to customer calls or analyzing support tickets. When filing a complaint, or a call to support, the customer is showing that he cares about the product and is willing to initiate the conversation.

Solving customer problems with the teams is the best way to learn about them, but it is also the best antidote against the Big Company Disease. It helps focus people on customers over processes, it fosters teamwork across the company, it focuses management on results rather than power plays, and helps clarify which technologies are worth investing in.

🕪 Time to practice

CUSTOMER BOARD

Starting from customer complaints, or studying the last support requests with your customer service agents, you can set up a "customer board" to solve specific customer problems together. For instance, in a marketing agency producing videos you could find the following board:

Date	Customer	Problem
March 11	John Doe / xxx	Requests major changes on the marketing video before publishing because it does not reflect the brand's identity

Time to practice

Note that this also applies to internal customers if you are the head of a specific department.

On a strategic level you are working on two things:

- Putting customers at the center of everyone's attention, to fight the Big Company Disease
- Getting a deeper understanding of who your customers are and where they are heading. In this case the way we design branding elements in our service is not sufficient for this customer.

Probable Causes	Countermeasure	Result
We only talk about target demographics and performance goals during the initial discussions with customers	[Alan / March 14] During the next brief, show a few sample videos to the customer to have a discussion about branding	Next video accepted first time

BEWARE OF THE QUICK FIX

Solving customer problems can be fruitless as a learning exercise if we jump to solutions too quickly.

There are three main kinds of misconceptions to avoid:

- **Proposing a solution when we don't all agree on the problem**. For instance the CTO proposes to change a piece of technology to improve stability while the VP of engineering proposes to hire a pair of product managers to speed up development. Are we talking about a quality problem or a productivity problem?

- **Proposing a solution based on an imagined cause.** This could be changing the layout and graphics of a landing page to increase conversions when in reality customers are turned off by misleading copy.

- **Proposing a solution without being aware of its unintended consequences.** For instance, changing the ticketing software used by a support team to get better reporting capabilities, when the new tool makes the job more difficult for agents and causes a significant hit to productivity.

5

THE PRACTICE

FIND 2

ACTING ON MISCONCEPTIONS

The Chief Operating Officer in charge of customer support noticed several times that tickets had been left behind and customers complained that they had to wait several weeks for help.

Then she has an idea. She thinks that with a new ticket management tool and a small change in the ticketing process, the processing would be much more efficient. She manages to convince her managers and some of her colleagues to adopt a new tool, but after a few weeks spent on a big implementation project she notices that not all her colleagues are using it and that customers continue to complain. Her first reaction is to think that the company is resistant to change, but after a while she realizes three things:

— The initial problem, the fact that tickets are lying around for weeks, is not really solved even with colleagues who play the game.

— Part of the team is destabilized by the introduction of the new tool

— Other problems have emerged, for example reporting is now much more difficult for the team leader.

The problem is clear, even though it is not quantified; it is a problem of lead time—the time between the customer request and the response.

She jumps to an action without having confirmed the cause. Why do these specific tickets take longer?
From this point the logic is based on assumptions, and probably off the mark. The actions are therefore pointless.

These are typical outcomes of a solution implemented for no solid reason.

THINK AS A SCIENTIST: THE PDCA CYCLE

The art of thinking straight has been honed for over a few hundred centuries. The main contribution of lean thinking is to bring everyone in the company to use it every day at work.

Here is the sequence of questions that you can use whenever you are trying to improve something.

What did we learn? How can we make sure that we do not revert to the same problem in the future? **ACT**

In what cases does the change work, and in what cases does it not work? **CHECK**

What is the problem we are trying to solve?

What is the current situation? At what point does this situation differ from the standard case?

What are the possible root causes of the abnormalities, apart from those which come to mind immediately? How can we confirm these causes before changing anything?

PLAN (1) What is the smallest change we could make to address the root cause?

DO (2) Are we implementing the simplest change and doing it as quickly as possible?

Did we get the agreement of all the people involved?

PDCA THINKING IN ACTION

The chief operating officer (COO) in charge of customer support notices that some tickets have been waiting for several weeks, causing customer complaints. She decides to clarify the problem, counting cases to see how the phenomenon evolves over time.

Digging in her ticketing tool she discovers that out of the approximately 800 tickets closed each week, 60 are processed in more than 15 days. She discusses it with her colleagues, who are surprised at the extent of the problem and recognize that it is an appropriate subject to deal with.

The team proposes to recruit one or two additional people, but the COO does not get distracted so easily. She first studies concrete cases to understand precisely what it is all about. It's a matter of lead time, so she draws a graph on which she notes the steps and dates of the complete process for a dozen of these tickets, from creation to closing. For most of them, she asks some questions to her colleagues in order to reconstruct the story. After one or two hours of investigation, two families emerge. In the first one, it happens that the person in charge of these tickets is outside the team and only takes care of them about once a week, when she has sufficient time. The second family of tickets represents situations in which the agents do not have the necessary information and the customer takes time to answer.

She focuses on the first family of cases. Why are some of the tickets being assigned to someone outside the team? Discussing with the person in question, she learns that they are related to an old back-office application for which it was thought that the support team was unable to respond. She asks her colleagues and learns that this is not true: two of them are familiar with this application.

Root cause hypothesis

A root cause of these cases is therefore that we have a problem in the way tickets are routed because the skills of agents are not well known.

Root cause confirmed

The root cause being confirmed, she proceeds to find a countermeasure. The two people who are familiar with the old back-office system have proposed to modify the routing of these tickets so that they are directly assigned to them.

In the following days she visits the people involved in the issue to make sure that the countermeasures are properly implemented. These actions are not yet definitive; they are experimental. At this stage she tries things quickly to see what works and what doesn't.

Counter-measure

As the actions are tested, she measures the results. She notes that the number of tickets closed in more than 15 days is indeed decreasing, but not as much as she thought. At the same time, she continues to investigate other root causes and test other actions.

Check

ROOTING OUT MISCONCEPTIONS

From a learning perspective, the goal of problem-solving is to improve our understanding of our business. In cognitive terms, this understanding takes the form of a mental model or a causal map: how different factors influence specific outcomes. The ultimate goal of problem-solving is to uncover the factors that we are not controlling that keeps limiting our performance.

For this reason, the most important part of the PDCA cycle is finding the root causes.

This is usually done by repeatedly asking "why?" This creates a causal tree as shown in the adjacent figure.

But what should you look for in this investigation? When should you stop? As a rule of thumb, you can explore causes while trying to answer the question:

> **"What is the mistake we keep repeating that creates this problem?"**

Do not get stuck on one or two obvious causes. You want to expand your thinking, imagine very different plausible explanations for what is happening.

The page takes
4s to load
instead of 1s

Why?  Why?

The CSS and HTML files are not compressed

3 images weigh more than 4Mo even though they occupy a small area on the page

Why?

Why?

The developer did not specify it in the build script

We explain nothing of this sort to the user who uploads the file, and make nothing to prevent these errors from happening

Why?

We don't train developers to create pages that load fast

WRITING PROBLEM SOLVING REPORTS DOWN

Solving problems does not necessarily result in learning. In a typical company, myriads of problems are solved every day without the company learning anything at all in the process.

To speed up learning, you need to create the opportunity for people to have a discussion about how they went about solving the problem—a discussion about their thinking.

This discussion will be much more effective if the process of their thinking is written down.

Two problem-solving reports are proposed here—one for day-to-day, small improvements, and another, the A3 report, for more involved investigations.

There are no specific guidelines on how the reports should be filled out, other than this one: it is up to the writer to find how to convey his ideas the most clearly.

It would be a mistake to standardize in too much detail how these documents should be filled in, since the whole purpose of the exercise is to see what the writer has in mind.

Another mistake to avoid is asking people for fill out these reports but then having no discussion about it with them. This is a sure way to turn a learning tool into a hollow, soul-draining process. What is written in the reports is not what really counts—it is the quality of the discussion about the report that does. There should be a discussion to see if we agree on:

— The problem we want to solve
— The method to get there

Date	Who	Problem	Probable causes	Counter-measure	Result

Daily problem solving

Title		Author	Date
Problem	**Countermeasures**		
Analysis			
	Results		
Target			
Hypotheses of causes	**Learnings**		

A3 problem solving report used by managers
to communicate on improvement projects

ALL COOL AND RATIONAL, NO FEELINGS?

Reading about scientific thinking might leave you wondering if there is no place for human emotion in a lean approach. Additionally, you will find many cases, when going through your first PDCA cycles, where your first instinct will be to settle on causes like "they don't get along" or "lack of motivation."

The first reason we look for hard facts is that they are often the true root causes. If, for instance, a sales representative is getting emotional because he is missing quota for the third quarter in a row, and at the same time he does not know how to craft good sales proposals, no amount of cajoling will help him succeed. You would be working on the symptoms, not the causes.

The same holds true for two teams that don't work well together. You would be better off making sure they both know what the end customer wants, how both teams contribute, and what they needed to exchange together, before spending too much time on the psychology and mediation of the situation.

Once these topics are taken care of, feelings and relationships are of course critical—you won't go far with unmotivated people who don't like to work with each other. But then, the question for you would be: how do you develop your own skills in this area? Are you just following your instincts (i.e., be amateurish), or do you make the effort to learn what other people have discovered over the past centuries about getting agreement at work?

5

THE PRACTICE

FIND 2

SOLVING PROBLEMS TO DISCOVER VALUE

The first customer problems you will probably uncover reveal the low-hanging fruits: mistakes that no one noticed before but now stand in the open, waiting to get fixed.

Resolving these problems will raise performance a bit, and this is not to be dismissed since it will make life that much easier for customers and it will develop people in the process.

But what you are looking for, though, is the deeper set of problems that reflect the customer perception of your products.

For instance, once your web application's few bugs and performance issues are fixed, you realize that your reports are missing important information that would suddenly make your product a must-have for some customers. Or better yet, you discover unresolved customer problems that help orient the design of the next generation of your product.

At this stage, it's not about superficial fixes anymore: it becomes a strategy for a bottomless source of customer insights, a never-ending rediscovery of value that keeps the company relevant over time.

5 | THE PRACTICE | FIND | 2

FIND

Craft the strategy from the ground up

3 MAKE VALUE FLOW

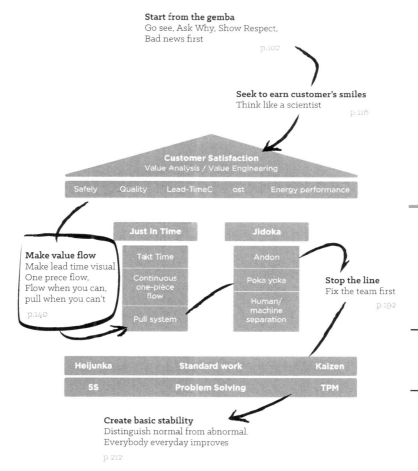

MAKE VALUE FLOW

The second dimension of the lean strategy is the acceleration of value, which is achieved through a never-ending reduction of lead time—the time from a customer request to the final delivery:

Reducing the lead time gives the company a competitive edge because customers will always prefer the fastest delivery, and they are often willing to pay extra for it. Lead-time reduction is therefore a top-line improvement strategy.

But it is also a potent lever for bottom-line performance. **Toyota's insight is that delays are the physical representation of problems which occur across the value stream.** Every mistake, every rework, every gap in coordination translates into extra delays from the customer perspective.

Lead-time reduction acts as a powerful detox plan: problems are surfaced, ready to be resolved.

As problems are eliminated and lead time is reduced, the financial health of the company improves:

— With shorter lead times, the business can function with less cash.
— With fewer problems, operational costs decrease.

But above all, the discipline of lead-time reduction creates a rich environment for people to learn from, digging into the root causes of problems surfaced daily. It also creates the conditions for good teamwork, because it cuts across silos and brings people to better collaborate with other teams across the company. As such, lead-time reduction is the ultimate weapon against the Big Company Disease.

To foster learning in your company, you need to develop your own skills in lead-time reduction. It starts with pursuing the ideal state of flow: value flying from one step of the process to the next, without pause, reaching the customer as fast as possible.

A COMPANY IS A SET OF FLOWS

Thinking in terms of lead time applies to the whole company once you learn to see it as a large collection of intertwined flows. For instance, here are a few typical flows in an e-commerce company:

Customer purchase	⏰ —	Product selection —	Purchase —
Product sourcing	⏰ —	New product selection —	Supplier sourcing —
Recruitment	⏰ —	Job definition —	Candidate sourcing —

For this reason, TPS thinking applies to every part of the company.

Sales   Marketing   Operations   Logistics

————— Expedition — Transport — Delivery ⟶|

————— Negotiation — Product selection — Catalog update ⟶|

————— Candidate selection — Negotiation & Contracting — Onboarding ⟶|

Product development　　**Customer support**　　**HR**　　etc.

MAKE LEAD TIME VISUAL

To start practicing, you can pick a process you are responsible for in your company and try to reduce its lead time by following the next steps.

As a starting point, you need to see what is going on. At what step in the process do specific customer requests occur? Which ones are stagnating? Why?

The key here is to avoid thinking in terms of averages. Once averaged out, the data loses its most valuable information.

What you need is a simple, visual system in place to see individual customer requests and their corresponding lead time at a glance on the gemba, so that you can dig deep into a few cases.

This is the purpose of kanban.

5
THE PRACTICE
FIND
3

Time to practice

KANBAN

A kanban is a simple production signal, a kind of ticket used to purchase something from an upstream process. It can be a ticket created by a customer to "order" an answer from a customer support service, a card filled by a product manager to "order" a feature from a tech team, or a job description sent to the recruitment team to "order" a new hire.

Kanban may take many forms, paper or electronic. The information and layout will change from one context to the next, depending on what the team is learning at the moment. What is important is that you can see at a glance all the current requests with these details:

— **Who is the customer?**
— **What is being requested?**
— **When was the request emitted?**
— **Who is processing it right now, or who is going to process it?**

Note that kanban is not a tool to organize production. Kanban is an education tool whose main purpose is to make the situation visible. Like a radioactive marker in the body, it is a tool designed to reveal how value is flowing across a system. As such, it loses its edge as soon as you stop using it to learn about what is causing delays in the value creation flow.

Time to practice

You can set up a kanban system right now, with a crucial tip: do not overthink it. Trying something simple today is much better than planning a full system for the future. If you already have a ticketing system in place, start with it. If there is nothing, a simple spreadsheet or a few Post-it Notes are sufficient to start with. You really don't need that super new computer thing that will take months to implement.

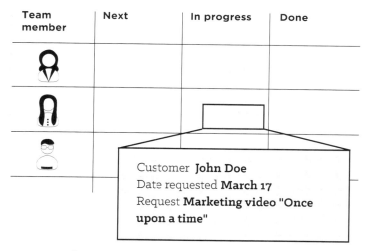

Production flow shown as individual swim lanes

Time to practice

Team member	Customer	Date requested	Request
👤	John Doe	March 17	Marketing video "Once upon a time"
👤	Sofia Smith	Feb 24	Newsletter "Spring collection"
👤	Jeff Adler	Jan 18	Landing page "Spring outfits"

A list of requests in a ticketing system

	Resp.	Jan	
Design website prototype	👤	⊢―――	
Launch website	👤		
Launch acquisition campaign	👤		

Milestones for a project

page 150

Time to practice

	Feb	Mar	Apr	Comments
	●			
		○ ▲		
		○	△	

○ Planned　● Delivered on time　△ Expected late　▲ Delivered late

STUDYING KANBAN

Kanban allows everyone, from team members to top management, to see what is going on in the company. For each individual customer, there is absolute clarity on what the promise was and what reality is.

This is a fundamental lean tool, to the point that **there is no lean without kanban**. It is therefore a key focus of attention during your gemba walks.

You can start studying kanbans right away by exploring simple questions:

- **Is it normal for the team to be working on this item now?**

- **Why is this request taking longer?** You can dive into one or two cases, trying to reconstruct the sequence of events that led to the delay.

As for customer issues, you are trying to think as a scientist. What is the gap in our understanding? What is the mistake that we keep repeating that leads to this delay? The PDCA questions are highly relevant here.

Time to practice

DAILY PROBLEM SOLVING

Studying kanbans day after day will uncover a myriad problems. The role of management is to step in and help solve them, one at a time, to better understand the business and create the conditions for the teams to succeed.

A common practice is to use the table below to track problems as they are solved, day after day.

Date	Who	Problem	Probable Causes
April 3	Jane Smith	2 hours late to deploy the website because the security certificate had expired	We never check the expiration dates of our assets.

↓ What is the obstacle?

↓ What are our hypothesis? How do we confirm them?

Time to practice

To get the most out of this practice:

— Avoid solving problems in meetings with a large team. It is much more practical and efficient to work on the gemba with one or two people directly involved in the situation.

— Display this table in the team's workspace so that 1/ the team becomes familiar with PDCA thinking and sees that its situation is improving, and 2/ management can have discussions about improvement with the team during its gemba walks.

— Have team members briefly present the problem solving to the team, for instance during daily meetings.

Countermeasure	Result
[Sergio / April 5] Replaced the certificate	Website deployed + Discovered that the cache management system license was also about to expire
[Alan / April 6] Set up a calendar to check the web server assets	

What is the simplest thing we can try to remove the obstacle?

DIGGING DEEPER

As you gain a better understanding of your operations, you will be able to gather the low-hanging fruit, improve the situation for a few customers, and deepen your relationship with team members.

To go further, though, you need to develop your own expertise in lead time reduction—accelerating flows in a system as complex as a company requires specific skills.

The following sections describe what you need to know to become a proficient lead time reducer:

- How to analyze lead time
- How to identify the products delivered by the process
- How to analyze the causes of variability
- How to align all the process steps on the same cadence
- How to avoid batches and strive towards the ideal of one-piece flow
- How to setup a pull system when continuous one-piece flow is not attainable

Note that you don't need to try everything at once—that could be overwhelming, and would cause lots of resistance.

It is much better to make progress step-by-step.
It starts with getting to know the enemy: what is lead time made of?

THE ANATOMY OF LEAD TIME

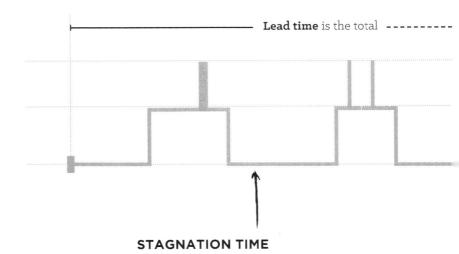

Lead time is the total

STAGNATION TIME

Stagnation time is when the piece is left untouched, waiting for the next step in the process. In most processes stagnation time amounts to over 80 percent of the lead-time. It is the first target of a lead time reduction effort, meaning that lead time can be drastically reduced by arranging how pieces flow from one step of the process to the next, and without changing anything in the way work is performed by people or machines at a specific point in the process.

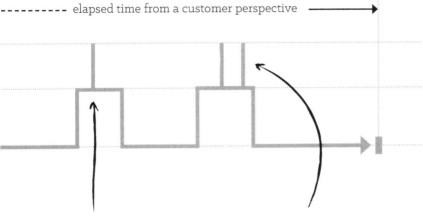

TOUCH TIME

Touch time is when the piece is being processed by a person or a machine. This can be reduced further in a second time, by rethinking the way work is done in such a way that only value-added actions are performed.

VALUE-ADDED TIME

The moment when the piece is actually transformed and gains value in the eyes of the customer.

In software development, when creating a specification document, part of the time is value-added (shaping up the solution, which has a very direct impact on the final product) and part of the time is non-value added (the very act of writing it down, which customers themselves do not need).

THE ULTIMATE GOAL: JUST-IN-TIME

In order to achieve the shortest possible lead time, with no stagnation and no waste of time, everyone in the company needs to work in sync. For instance, when writing an article for an online publication, the graphic designer, copywriter and web designer would need to coordinate their actions as follows:

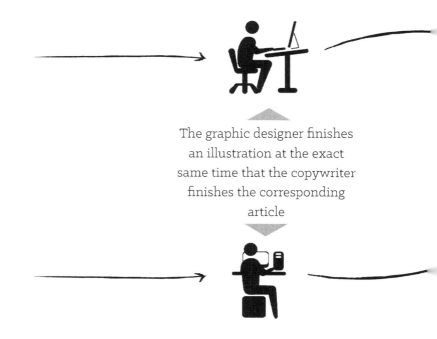

The graphic designer finishes an illustration at the exact same time that the copywriter finishes the corresponding article

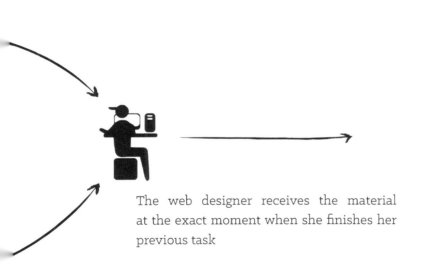

The web designer receives the material at the exact moment when she finishes her previous task

These are the conditions of **Just-in-Time**: everyone doing exactly what is needed, in the amount needed, at the precise moment when it is needed.

DEALING WITH VARIABILITY

Maintaining the conditions of Just-in-Time consistently across the company seems like an impossible feat. People are working on many different things, tasks seldom repeat in the same way, mistakes are made which require repairing, and frequent interruptions increase the general level of chaos.

At first, this high level of variability could be seen as the hallmark of a modern, dynamic company. But it comes with a price: excessive variability inhibits learning and prevents optimization, resulting into longer lead times and higher costs.

Companies evolve in a turbulent environment—changes in customer demand, in work practices, in technology, etc. The job of management is to create the right conditions of stability inside the company, so that people can work and learn efficiently enough to make visible progress.

**Dealing with variation consumes time
and energy, and reduces profitability**

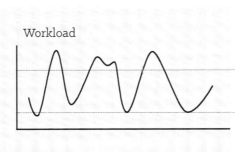

If you staff for for this level of activity, you lose money during the valleys

If you staff for this level of activity, people and customers suffer during the peaks

As a first step of this journey, there are four myths to debunk.

MISCONCEPTIONS ABOUT VARIABILITY

IT FOSTERS CREATIVITY!

Reacting to unexpected situations does require some creativity. The real question, though, is what remains of this creativity after the fact. In most cases, nothing. The idea will not be used later because the conditions will have changed.

From a lean perspective, just reacting to random events is a waste of people's intelligence and time. A much better use of their capabilities is understanding the causes of variation and finding creative approaches to improve known, controlled activities.

IT MAKES WORK MORE INTERESTING!

It only does for a while; after a few months, constant variation becomes the new normal, and people get bored.

Durable motivation comes from a sense of progress, and progress is achieved by improving step by step a sufficiently stable activity.

IT'S WHAT SEPARATES US FROM MACHINES!

What separates us from machines is above all our ability to understand a system and find ideas for improvement.

A counterintuitive thing about stability is that we look for ways to standardise activities so that we can think about them and change them.

We are just looking for a different kind of variation: controlled improvement over chaotic reaction.

IT'S WHAT FLEXIBILITY AND AGILITY ARE ABOUT!

As variability increases, people spend more and more time reacting to it and lead time increases for customers. From the outside, the company is just slow, not agile.

Real agility is the result of a trade-off: accepting the variable demands of customers while maintaining sufficient stability internally to execute controlled processes very fast.

PROTECT, STABILIZE AND OPTIMIZE

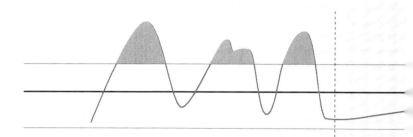

To reduce variability and optimize a system, the correct improvement sequence consists in resolving problems in that order:

1. OVERBURDEN

As people and machines are working above their capabilities, their performance drops considerably—much like overloaded roads lead to traffic congestion.
This happens with long working days, excessive workloads or very difficult tasks. It also may be an emotional overburden, with employees dealing with abusive customers or managers.

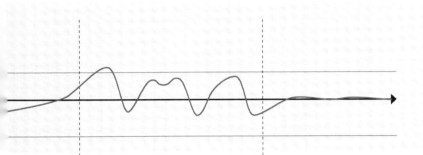

2. VARIABILITY

Variability prevents improvements from sticking over time, and thus impedes progress.

It can take different forms: a variable workload from one day to the next, changing tasks, different equipment for the same tasks, different ways to do the same task, etc.

3. WASTE

Waste is all the effort spent by people and machines that does not translate into creating value for customers.

It can be producing items that nobody expects, fixing defects, moving information or products from one person to the next, waiting for someone or something, switching contexts, etc.

VARIABILITY ANALYSIS

You can study the causes of variability of a dozen specific cases along five dimensions, called the "5M", and represent these causes using a fishbone diagram:

MAN

Ron was sick and Jane didn't know how to use the new machine

MATERIAL

The customer request did not specify the address of the server that needed repairing

METHOD

The upgrade procedure contained an erroneous deletion command which resulted in user data loss

Time to practice

MACHINE

The security certificate of the web server expired on Saturday night

⟶ **ABNORMALITY**

MOTHER NATURE

The unprecedented snowstorm caused an 8-hour electricity shortage, and we couldn't get out to buy fuel

CREATING THE CONDITIONS OF JUST-IN-TIME

The TPS is a blueprint for creating the conditions of Just-in-Time in the face of high variability.

It starts with three principles :

- **Takt time:** Align all activities on a shared, constant drumbeat
- **Continuous one-piece flow:** Strive to flow products from one step to the next, item by item, without pausing or backtracking
- **Pull system:** At places in the process where continuous flow is not possible, only produce when the next step in the process is requesting it.

Keep in mind that these are just starting points. Since TPS is a system, these principles all depend on the rest of the TPS. It all starts with a fundamental question: what do you produce?

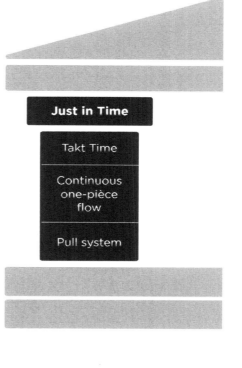

Time to practice

PRODUCT MIX

One of the first causes of variability is the variety of the products to be made. At the post office, the clerk spends much more time sending a parcel to a foreign country than selling a standard set of stamps.

To be able to accelerate your flows, you need to be very clear on your products, and have an idea of the daily, weekly or monthly volumes of each product. The key point here is to avoid confusing activities (e.g. extracting data) and products (a report). When thinking in terms of flows, activities are steps in a value creation process that lead to the delivery of a final product.

For instance a ride-sharing service produces rides of different kinds. A marketing team produces various types of content, with a common outcome which is the visibility of the brand. A customer service department produces answers to different families of questions. You can think of these outputs as the equivalent of pieces in a factory.

Time to practice

The basic model:

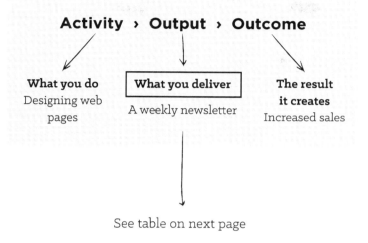

See table on next page

◐ Time to practice

You can fill the table below to clarify the various types of products made by your teams.

Products	Vol.	Process steps		
		Research	Copy	Illustration
Newsletter	1	x	x	x
Video	4	x	x	x
Landing page	12	x	x	x
...				

It is best to approach the lead time reduction effort product by product, starting with the highest volumes. Working one product at a time will make things easier, and choosing the high volume one first will have the greatest impact.

Depending on the volumes and the size of the team, you may even consider temporarily dedicating some people to this specific process—in the example below, two people could focus on building landing pages.

Time to practice

...	Video editing	Web design	Targetting	Ads
		x	x	x
	x			x
		x		x

WORKING IN SYNC

The next phenomenon to address is the unevenness of workloads, both from one day to the next and along the value-creation process.

Levelling workload over time can be done by averaging the daily or weekly volume of products and creating a constant rhythm of production. This constant pace is called "takt" (German for the rhythm of the metronome), which is the average time between the sale of two products. For instance, if you need to recruit 100 people this year, you should expect a new hire every 2.5 days. In other words, the company "purchases" a new hire every 2.5 days to the recruitment team.

This leaves unevenness of workload between the various steps of the process. Uneven processing times create two kinds of inefficiencies:

- —— If the downstream process takes less time it will cause unfinished items (specifications, articles, code, sales proposals, etc.) to stagnate, waiting for the slower activity to complete.
- —— If the downstream process takes more time, the upstream process will waste time waiting or finding another task.

The most efficient situation is therefore one where every step of the process takes exactly the same time, at the pace of customer purchases. In other words, when everybody works at takt time.

The takt is a fundamental tool for designing a process. For instance if it takes on average twice as long to code a feature than to design it, you need twice as many developers as product managers.

The difference in processing time creates stagnation

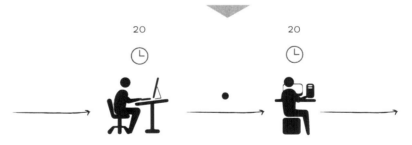

In an ideal situation, all the steps in the process should take the same time, aligned with customer demand

TAKT TIME

To stabilize the activity and uncover potential for improvement, you can compute the takt time for your activity and study the average time at each step of the process.

$$\text{Takt} = \frac{\text{Duration of period}}{\text{\# items sold in period}}$$

For instance,

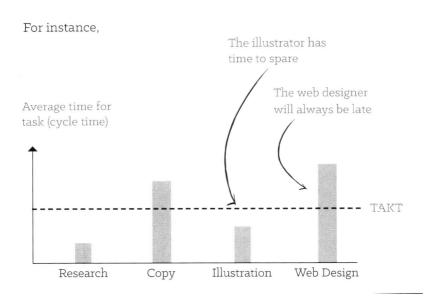

Time to practice

What is the takt time for your process?
What is the cycle time at each step?
What do you learn?

IT DEPENDS!

When trying to evaluate the takt time or the cycle of an activity, or when performing the exercises in this book, you will often find that the answer is not clear because "it depends". Workloads vary from one day to the other, cycle time depends on the request and who is performing the job, and so on.

It would be a mistake to dismiss these questions thinking that it only applies to repeating industrial operations.

Feel comfortable starting with ballpark estimates and refining your analysis over time, step by step. This is part of the learning journey. Trying to better understand these numbers will lead you to clarify your products, the factors of variability, etc.

A deep understanding of the causes of variation in the activity is the difference between the amateur and the pro.

5

THE PRACTICE

FIND 3

BATCHES LEAD TO STAGNATION

After a mismatch in work cycle times, a second major cause of stagnation is people working on batches of items.

This happens, for instance, when product managers write a complete specification, with many different features, before sending everything to developers. From the perspective of an individual feature, most of the time is spent waiting for the other features being completed before reaching developers.

A video production team that sets up a large shooting session that will give birth to 20 short sequences, then editing all of them at once, is also working in batches.

Working in batches lengthens lead times, but it also hides problems with quality. If the first item contains a defect, it will only be visible when the whole batch reaches the next step in the process— leading to all the items in the batch needing rework.

Working on several items at once also happens frequently when people are stuck. You certainly experience it every day yourself; you start a task, then get stuck because you lack some piece of information, then switch to another task and so on.

However, people work best when they can proceed one piece at a time with no hassle and no interruption. Juggling with multiple tasks hides the problems that prevent people from finishing them, leads to cognitive fatigue, and reduces quality and productivity.

A fundamental goal in lead-time reduction is therefore to achieve the ideal of one-piece flow.

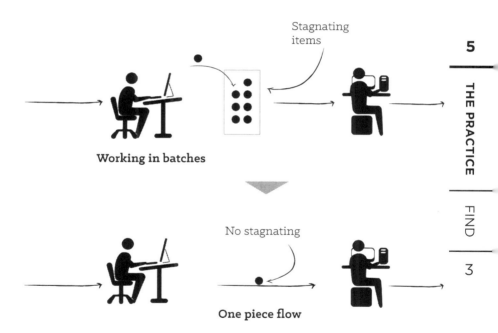

CONTINUOUS ONE-PIECE FLOW

One-piece flow—completing every item before moving to the next one—is a powerful approach for revealing obstacles, and thus finding ideas for improvement.

Just imposing one-piece flow—"you shall all do one thing at a time"—is completely missing the point. The goal remains to learn, so every situation where a person is juggling with several tasks is a great opportunity to start a conversation and ask, "What happened?"

You can therefore organize your kanban in such a way that this situation becomes visible, and then start analyzing and trying to solve these problems. This is rich material for PDCA thinking.

The starting point is quite simple.

Time to practice

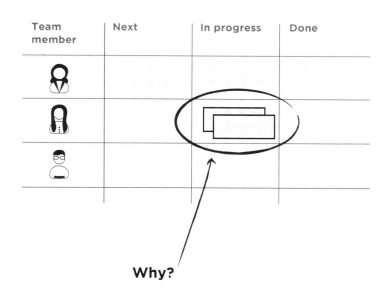

FLOW WHEN YOU CAN, PULL WHEN YOU CAN'T

There is very little chance that you will be able to achieve a state of continuous one-piece flow in your process—everyone at each step working at takt time, with no stagnation in between. Customer demand fluctuates, workloads are different, products are varied and many factors cause interruptions every day.

One-piece flow is a destination, a north star. Every change that brings you closer to it is a good thing, every change that brings you farther is worth having a closer look at.

When one-piece flow is not possible, you still need to find a way to avoid overproduction—someone who keeps producing even when the person downstream is already busy. This would be a waste of the person's time, resulting in stagnation.

This happens, for instance, in software development, when product owners or product managers keep piling up feature specifications while software developers cannot keep the pace. These product managers could make better use of their time on other activities—finding ways to help developers, performing user tests, etc.

A proven way to manage this situation is to establish a pull system, as shown in the right-hand figure. In such a system, the person upstream maintains a buffer of finished items—

for instance, a blog post, an illustration, a report. This is called a "shop stock," as if person A was filling a rack in a supermarket aisle. When the shop stock is considered full (usually an arbitrary number of items) it means that person B downstream is not keeping pace, and it becomes counterproductive for A to produce anymore.

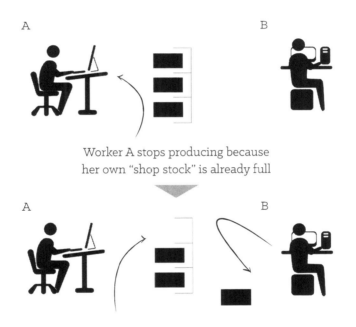

Worker A stops producing because her own "shop stock" is already full

As soon as B withdraws an item, the empty slot is a signal for A to start producing the next one, replenishing her shop stock

Time to practice

PULL SYSTEM

Building a pull system is a means for intensifying teamwork throughout the organization, each person becoming more aware of her interactions with her own customer: the next person in the process.

A pull system is therefore much more than a technique for limiting the amount of work in the process. To create pull, you can have a discussion with each individual in the process, trying to clarify:

— Who is your immediate customer?
  This can be an internal or external customer
— What items does he expect?
— What are the key points of a good item for him?
— At what frequency does he expect them?
— In what form? How could you make work easier for him?
— What is a reasonable amount of stock between you two, after which you would be better off stopping production of new items?

This should trigger in turn a discussion between the two colleagues. The same applies for the whole value chain

Time to practice

from the end customer to your own suppliers.

As each person is the customer of the previous person in the process, a currency is needed to "buy" products from the upstream processes; this is the role of kanban.

In a pull system, each person should have:

- **A prioritized list of the next kanban to process** (for instance in a ticketing system)
- **A personal "shop stock"** where she can make her products available to her own customers
- **A frequent discussion with her customers and her team leader about the quality of her products**

FLOWING FOR LEARNING

Keep in mind that the lead-time reduction techniques we have seen here—takt, flow, pull—are learning mechanisms. Trying to put everything in place will invariably reveal many obstacles and raise lots of questions, and this is precisely the point.

These principles are designed to encourage discussion and allow problems to surface every day. It is all part of the lean education system. Having everything in place is not a goal in itself—the goal is to develop people so that the company can deliver more value to customers.

For people to learn, you need to create feedback and discussions, stopping the production line when something interesting occurs to explore what quality means at each step of the process. This is the purpose of Jidoka.

5

THE PRACTICE

FIND

3

FIND

Craft the strategy from the ground up

4 STOP THE LINE

Start from the gemba
Go see, Ask Why, Show Respect,
Bad news first
p.102

Seek to earn customer's smiles
Think like a scientist
p.118

Customer Satisfaction
Value Analysis / Value Engineering

| Safely | Quality | Lead-Time | Cost | Energy performance |

Just in Time
- Takt Time
- Continuous one-piece flow
- Pull system

Jidoka
- Andon
- Poka yoka
- Human/machine separation

Make value flow
Make lead time visual
One prece flow,
Flow when you can,
pull when you can't
p.140

Stop the line
Fix the team first
p.192

| Heijunka | Standard work | Kaizen |
| 5S | Problem Solving | TPM |

Create basic stability
Distinguish normal from abnormal.
Everybody everyday improves
p.212

5 THE PRACTICE

FIND

4

STOP THE LINE

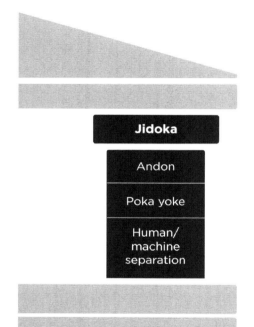

The constant need to reduce lead time to better satisfy customers creates a tension inside the company. Kanban acts as a signal to distribute this tension across the organization, helping people better work together to handle it. This is a source of progress, but can quickly become unbearable as problems arise and disrupt the normal flow of work.

For this reason, Just-in-Time cannot stand without its counterpart: Jidoka.

While Just-in-Time is the pillar of Teamwork, Jidoka is the pillar of Respect: helping each individual team member succeed every day. It is based on three main principles:

- **Andon:** Stop the line when an abnormal situation occurs and signal so that management can step in, react immediately, and help remove its root cause.
- **Poka yoke:** Create systems that prevent mistakes from being made so that work is less taxing and people can focus their attention on improving the system.
- **Human-machine separation:** Build tools that enhance people rather than control them.

Time to practice

ANDON:
THE PRACTICE OF STOP & FIX

Andon is a mechanism used by a team member or a machine to signal an abnormal situation - for instance a mistake in the copy to be integrated in a landing page, a web server with unusually high processor usage, or missing details in a specifications document.

Andon can take many forms. Within factories, it is often a chord hanging above the operators that can be easily pulled when needed, triggering a red light or a signal on a display. It can also be a large red button near a workstation. In an office, it can just be raising one's hand, sending a text message or typing "help" in a dedicated channel in the company's communication tool. It can be an automated email sent to you by a computer system.

To start putting in place such a system, you can start at your level: do you have a clear system in place where every person you support knows who to call when there is a problem? How to call? In what situations to do it ?

Are your automated systems designed and configured to raise alarms when an abnormal situation arises? Do people in charge of these alerts work to remove their root causes?

Time to practice

FIX THE TEAM FIRST

You may probably wonder: What happens if everyone starts asking for help every time they face an abnormal situation? Will the company come to a halt? Who will answer all those calls?

On the other hand, preventing these interactions from happening would result in leaving lots of improvement potential on the table.

The TPS relies on a specific solution for resolving this dilemma: team leaders.

Recent management research shows that people are happier, more productive, and learn faster in the context of small teams of four to eight people led by a team leader. In their groundbreaking book Nine Lies about Work, Marc Buckingham and Ashley Goodall have shown that people's experience in a company mostly depend on their daily work interactions with their peers and their team leader. You join a company and leave your team leader.

This requires a specific organizational model: a team of teams.

5

THE PRACTICE

FIND

4

A SCALABLE STRUCTURE OF TEAMS

The team leader structure provides a model for a scalable company: about every five additional people, a new team leader must be designated to lead the team.

The andon call does not stop at the team leader level though. Team leaders are themselves part of four to eight-people teams led by a group leader, and so on.

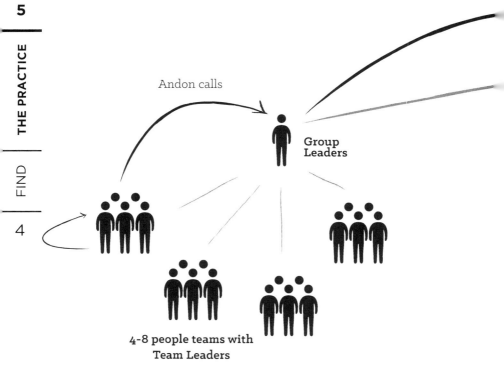

Even though it looks very similar at first, this is not an old Command & Control hierarchy. In a world of Orient & Support, this is a help chain: every leader is the teacher of the people she supports.

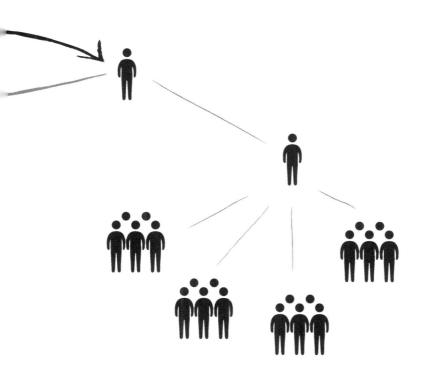

THE ROLE OF THE TEAM LEADER

The team leader role is the cornerstone of a lean organization. Good team leaders know how to foster a spirit of engagement and improvement in their teams.

But in most companies, people become team leaders without much training. The typical counterproductive leadership habits they adopt include:

— Doing the work in place of the team members, leaving no one to actually take care of the team

— Micromanaging the team members, imposing their own work methods

— Being totally absent from day-to-day operations, speeding from one meeting to the next

— Spending time allocating work to team members or coordinating activities (in a lean organization, this is the role of kanban)

A key role of the executive team is to spot, promote, and develop good team leaders.

Team leaders are not managers. They have a mainly operational role, and are fully involved in the day-to-day life of their team.

How do you spot the next team leaders? By going to the gemba and doing the exercises in this book. You will soon discover people who stand out.

— Their teammates turn to them when they need help.
— They care about the work and the company.
— They are competent, even if they are not the best technicians.

Once selected, you need to train them to become good leaders. The table on next page lists the main activities of a lean team leader.

For them to be effective, you need to give team leaders sufficient time to do their job. As a rule of thumb, the team leader of a four to eight-person team should be able to spend 50 percent of his time on the activities listed in this table.

Visualize	Make the activity visual so that each team member knows the team's goals, how to contribute, and what problems arise. This starts with setting up and maintaining a kanban.
Support	Respond to andon calls to help individual team members deal with abnormalities. Hold weekly one-on-one meetings with each team member to discuss priorities and help them succeed in their job.
Escalate	Perform andon calls to the group leader for larger problems.
Train	Create the work standards and training material, and hold short weekly training sessions with individual team members.
Maintain	Help team members make sure their work environment is always in good condition for doing quality work without hassle.
Improve	Lead day to day problem solving and engage all the team in an improvement project. This is called Kaizen, and described in the Form phase later in this book.

Responsibilities of a Team Leader

5

THE PRACTICE

FIND

4

Time to practice

RED BINS

The goal of the andon system is twofold: helping team members and developing attention to quality at each step of the process.

As people become clear on quality key points, they will uncover defects in many intermediary and final artifacts: mistakes in marketing copy, mistakes in product listings, incoherent or incomplete feature specifications, software bugs, etc. These are rich sources of learning.

A key practice in this area is that of the "red bins" review. This comes from the industry, where defective parts are put away in special (red) containers for further study.
To use red bins in your context, you can:

—— Identify what "defects" mean in your activity.

—— Agree with the team on a place where defective items can be placed. This might be a physical container, but also a shared folder, or tagged elements in a database.

—— During your next gemba walks, spend some time with the team leader analyzing the root causes of these defects, and try simple PDCA experiments to eliminate them.

Time to practice

1. A team member or a machine detects a defect

2. The defective part is put aside in a special container: the red bin

3. The team member and the team leader analyze the root cause of the defect to prevent its recurrence

POKA YOKE

When analyzing defects while responding to andon calls or studying red bins, you will probably find out that they are due to mistakes made by team members during moments of inattention.

It would be tempting to react by adding more control points and putting more pressure on people to double-check their work, but that would result in more waste—the cognitive overload of additional inspection work.

A more respectful and efficient way to manage this situation would be to invent error-proof systems.
Some examples of common, modern error-proof systems include:

— USB cables that can be plugged only in the correct position and the right type of plugs

— User interface elements such as date pickers that make it impossible to input an invalid date

— Strongly typed programming languages which prevent functions from being called with a wrong type of parameter, etc.

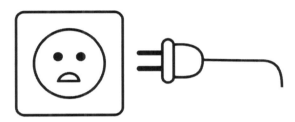

HUMAN-MACHINE - SEPARATION

Another way to help individuals do quality work is working with the help of machines. The last component of Jidoka is referred to as "autonomation" or "automation with a human touch."

Automation is all the rage now, widely seen as the main lever of productivity in modern companies. This is nothing new, as companies have been looking for a competitive advantage by betting on major advances in automation for the past 150 years.

The dark side of automation, though, is when the machines fail, causing major quality issues or interruptions. Managers end up recruiting people to fix the defects or deal with the frequent breakups, resulting in an overall cost increase for the activity.

The other dark side of automation is the possible degradation of work conditions for the workers. This was true in the factories of the early 1900s, and remains true nowadays in situations where computerized workflows treat humans as data entry interfaces, or where people must spend hours checking that the machine is not stopping or producing defects. This is a major waste of human intelligence.

The goal here is not to reject automation. The Lean Strategy does involve pursuing automation as much as possible, with the aim of relieving humans from repetitive tasks so that they can exert their intelligence on different tasks to create more value for society. The key is to design automated tools in such a way that humans and machines best collaborate together.

— Machines doing repetitive tasks with speed and precision

— Humans managing unexpected situations and performing improvements

A lean approach to automation unfolds like this:

— Engaging people who do the work to improve their activity until it is stable and well known

— Automating the repetitive parts and checking the impact on productivity

— Implementing automated checks so that the machine is able to detect abnormal situations on its own and perform andon calls. Humans can then do what they do best: solve unexpected problems.

This is a good observation point for one of your gemba walks: are people empowered by the tools provided by the company or are they controlled by these tools?

FIND

Craft the strategy from the ground up

5 CREATE BASIC STABILITY

Start from the gemba
Go see, Ask Why, Show Respect,
Bad news first
p.102

Seek to earn customer's smiles
Think like a scientist
p.118

Customer Satisfaction
Value Analysis / Value Engineering

| Safely | Quality | Lead-Time | Cost | Energy performance |

Just in Time
- Takt Time
- Continuous one-piece flow
- Pull system

Jidoka
- Andon
- Poka yoka
- Human/machine separation

Make value flow
Make lead time visual
One prece flow,
Flow when you can,
pull when you can't
p.140

Stop the line
Fix the team first
p.192

| Heijunka | Standard work | Kaizen |
| 5S | Problem Solving | TPM |

Create basic stability
Distinguish normal from abnormal.
Everybody everyday improves
p.212

5
THE PRACTICE
FIND
5

page 213

CREATE BASIC STABILITY

Solving problems to sustain the pulse of kanban and making the effort to pull the andon to draw the attention of management on abnormalities require committed employees. As a manager, how do you create the conditions for your people to be engaged at such a level?

TPS is a system for building motivation and commitment. The constant focus on the customer, the opportunities for teamwork that come from pursuing Just-in-Time, the availability for the team leader to help when needed, all these elements contribute to making every team member feel part of a close-knit team with a sense of purpose.

But all of this cannot last in a chaotic environment. It requires a foundation of stability.

The TPS identifies two levels of stability, further explored on the next pages

Customer Satisfaction

Just in Time — *Jidoka*

| Heijunka | Standard work | Kaizen |
| 5S | Problem Solving | TPM |

5 THE PRACTICE

FIND 5

1. STABILITY OF THE WORK ENVIRONMENT

How to develop a sense of ownership of one's work environment. It's about creating a bond of trust between employees and management.

2. STAYING IN CONTROL OF THE CHANGES

How to develop motivation, by doing varied tasks and taking the time to step back and reflect on one's work.

TRUST IN MANAGEMENT

Motivation at work starts with the basics: knowing what is expected of us and having the material means to succeed.

Material obstacles are motivation killers. A sales representative trying to hastily prepare a proposal for a customer gets mad when wasting time trying to find the latest version of the pricing calculator spreadsheet, rummaging through the shared folders of the sales team. The customer service agent suffers when trying to help a disgruntled customer over the phone when the communication is poor and the computer system freezes for three seconds at every click.

No amount of pep talk about becoming a learning organization or creating a different company will survive these mundane troubles for long. What makes these moments worse is when the employees themselves have no means to solve the problems. Ultimately, every additional problem of this kind erodes their trust in management.

The first step to motivating employees is taking care of the basics, by helping individual contributors take control of their working environment and solve the problems they face every day.

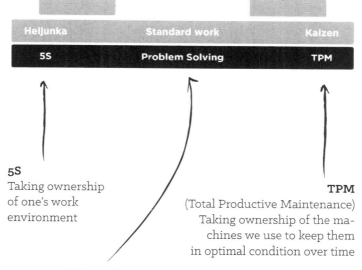

5S
Taking ownership of one's work environment

TPM
(Total Productive Maintenance) Taking ownership of the machines we use to keep them in optimal condition over time

Problem-Solving
Management steps in to help solve daily problems This is the role of the team leader, and your role during gemba walks

▥ Time to practice

TAKING OWNERSHIP WITH THE 5 "S"

Learning on the job starts with gaining a better mastery of one's workspace.

The workspace can be physical, for instance in a bike or scooter repair workshop. It can also be virtual, with office workers using an arrangement of files and tools on their computers. For software developers, it is not only the tooling; the structure and cleanliness of the whole codebase has a major impact on productivity.

You can practice workspace improvement starting with yours. The table on the right provides a list of questions based on the 5S framework.

You can then discuss with individual team members about how they organize theirs, why they do it that way, and how they could improve it further.

Beware of a classic trap: 5S is not an office cleanup program. The purpose of this approach is to think deeper about one's work, and therefore represents an important part of learning how to improve with standards.

Time to practice

Sort	What is sometimes used and what is never used in my workspace?
Straighten	How could I organize my work area in such a way that frequently used items are close at hand?
Shine	How can I make the workspace visual so that abnormal situations are immediately visible?
Standardize	How can I change my work habits in such a way that the workspace returns to normal after each use, without resorting to on-and-off cleanup sessions?
Sustain	As a team, how can we keep the discipline to do the first 4S over a long period of time?

MAKING WORK INTERESTING

Having the basic means to succeed is a prerequisite for motivation, but it is not sufficient. What makes work interesting is the right kind of variety:

— Switching between tasks we feel comfortable doing;
— Learning new things to do;
— Exploring novel ways to do our work.

This is the second level of the TPS foundation:

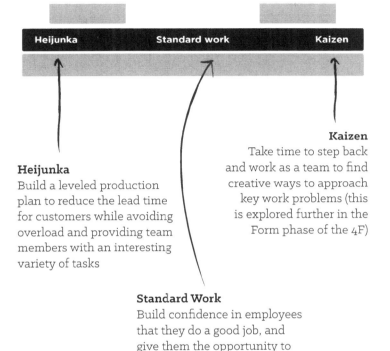

Heijunka
Build a leveled production plan to reduce the lead time for customers while avoiding overload and providing team members with an interesting variety of tasks

Standard Work
Build confidence in employees that they do a good job, and give them the opportunity to improve

Kaizen
Take time to step back and work as a team to find creative ways to approach key work problems (this is explored further in the Form phase of the 4F)

HEIJUNKA: THE IDEAL CUSTOMER

To organize production, you need to find the sweet spot on two different trade-offs:

Trade-off 1

If you change the workload every day to adjust to daily sales or production requirements, it better fits customers needs but it wreaks havoc in the teams during demand peaks and slowdowns:

Trade-off 2

If you work on a single product for a long period of time, it is best for productivity, but it makes work boring and makes lead time longer from a customer perspective:

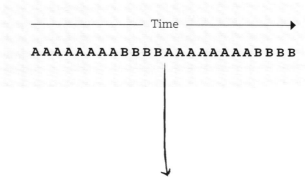

To resolve this dilemma, you build an ideal customer who shops a bit of everything every day, following a regular pattern. As a result, production is leveled both in terms of daily workload and production mix. Production is led by this ideal customer, greatly reducing variability:

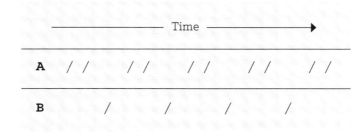

Time to practice

CREATING A LEVELED PRODUCTION PLAN

This plan, called a heijunka box, is composed as follows:

A row for each product
in the team's product mix

Time to practice

```
                    Columns representing units
                    of time - hours, days, weeks, months
                              ↓

              Mon  Tue  Wed  Thu  Fri  Mon  Tue  Wed
→  Video            /              /         /
   Landing page    /   /          /   /           /
                              ↑
              A recurring, leveled pattern of withdrawals
              from that ideal customer
```

Note that a leveled plan also provides a learning path for new team members, who can start with a first product, then a second, then alternate between more and more products as they grow their skills.

PUTTING IT ALL TOGETHER

With a leveled plan coupled with a pull system in which every person in the process withdraws what he needs from the upstream person, this produces the overall flow below:

1

Real customer demand is leveled to create an ideal customer who withdraws products according to a leveled plan

2

The leveled demand ripples across the company with the kanbans (production orders) of the pull system

3

Team leaders respond to andon calls to help team members, and they solve problems continually to foster learning and smooth production

4

As problems are addressed and people gain a greater mastery of their craft, the number of intermediary kanban (in-process stock) is lowered to reduce stagnation and shorten lead time, surfacing new problems to solve and promoting progress

DISTINGUISH NORMAL FROM ABNORMAL

To move from one task to the next with confidence, team members need a clear idea of how to do their job. The same is true for pulling the andon: they need to recognize a situation as abnormal before reacting to it. However, when solving problems on the gemba with your teams, you will soon be faced with situations where a team member lets a problem pass by without noticing it, he forgot a critical piece of information in a document, or he performed a task omitting an important step.

As problems pile up, you will probably—and rightfully—decide to clarify procedures and standards. The risk at this stage is to feed the bureaucracy that could accelerate the proliferation of the Big Company Disease. Instead of considering standards as prescriptive guides that control people's actions (Command & Control), you can think of standards as mechanisms that help people distinguish normal situations from abnormal ones and then use their best judgment (Orient & Support).

5

THE PRACTICE

FIND

STANDARDS THAT ORIENT & SUPPORT

HOW TO WRITE A LANDING PAGE

1. Copy and paste ad text in landing page header
2. Upload picture with at least 3 startup people from website ___
3. Add sales copy, 400 words
4. Add 4 testimonials from Twitter feed
5. Run spell-check
6. Add "Subscribe now" button
   (font size 20pt and button color #1268FF)
7. …

A procedure that takes control of the team member (Command & Control)

HOW TO WRITE A LANDING PAGE

Intention
Give visitors the information they are looking for and lead them to perform the intended action

Key Elements
— Headline: Concise and continuation of source email or ad
— Description: Link to the visitor problem / less than 500 words
— Social proof: Raving reviews from social media + icons from well-trusted websites
— Prominent call to action
— ...

Frequent Errors to Avoid
Spelling and grammar mistakes

A standard that helps the team member distinguish normal from abnormal to let her think by herself (Orient & Support)

Time to practice

STANDARDS

You don't need to write standards for everything, unless you really know what you are doing. The first thing to do is thus to write a list. What are the 10 most critical, elementary skills that the team or person should master?

You can then work with team members to clarify how they distinguish normal from abnormal situations when using these skills.

When writing a standard, you want three elements:

> **Why:** What is the intention / what is the expected outcome?
> **Key points:** What should you pay attention to, based on what we have learned so far?
> **Mistakes:** What usual errors should you check for?

When written, a standard should be as short as possible—consider a single sheet of paper as a maximum.

Written documents are just one possible form of standards. You can configure tools, create templates, design visuals that help team members distinguish easily what is normal and abnormal. The more visual and intuitive, the better.

Examples of standards

— A sample source code file that shows all the coding conventions of the team

— A checklist for a production release of your software

— The five points of a compelling customer support response, along with five correct and five incorrect examples, etc.

EVERYBODY EVERY DAY IMPROVES

The TPS is a blueprint for an ideal: a company where each contributor is 100 percent customer focused and doing value-added work, where everyone is working in sync at takt time, pull systems are humming along with few hiccups, team leaders are responding immediately to team members eager to pull the andon, and all this in a stable, controlled operation.

Compared to this, your company may feel like a mess.

The good news is that you have greatly developed your awareness of the incredible potential that lies before you. Now is the time to roll up your sleeves and keep moving forward, one gemba at a time, one PDCA cycle at a time. The key is to engage every member of the company, one by one, in this continuous improvement journey. The TPS acts as a north star in this effort.

But solving problems on the gemba, while paramount, is not enough. It is now time to climb in the helicopter to take a bird's-eye view of the business.

5

THE PRACTICE

FIND

FACE TO FRAME
———————

FACE

Grasp and cherish your real problems

Look for the elephant
page 242

Intensify collaboration
The obeya
page 244

Halve the bad, double the good
page 248

Plain english P&L
page 252

5
THE PRACTICE
FACE

FACE

The questions framed by the TPS in the Find phase of the 4F cycle are designed to give you deep insights into the fundamentals of your business:

- What turns customers away? How could you create more value for them to stay?
- What prevents the company from moving faster, and people from working better together?
- What prevents people for doing quality work every day?
- In what ways does the company prevent employees from succeeding at work and contributing their best ideas?

Some of the reasons are straightforward and quickly addressed. Others are more difficult to accept because they point to your own misconceptions or that of the executive team.

Face is about having the courage to accept this feedback and committing to change. It is about taking a step back and changing your mind on the business—and yourself.

5

THE PRACTICE

FACE

LOOK FOR THE ELEPHANT

Below the superficial blunders lie a few deep flaws in the company. These are usually obvious problems that everybody has learned to avoid talking about, mostly for fear of being punished one way or another. It is the elephant in the room, hidden in plain sight.

Examples of elephants:

- "We have lost our edge over the years, most of our teams are doing low-level, no value-added work that has brought customers to see us as the low performance choice."

- "We thought that we provided first class training to our employees, but in reality most of them are clueless and customers are starting to notice."

- "The new, cheaper technology of our competitors is less advanced than ours, but customers prefer theirs." Or a variant: "We have always seen ourselves as the cutting edge guys, but now we are the ones being disrupted by nimble youngsters."

"We are lagging behind because the CEO is a shoot-from-the-hip sales guy who has been hurting the R&D teams with random feature requests for years."»

Challenges are not only internal. What often happens is that the management team is so focused on internal politics, or so obsessed with its current product, that it does not realize that its context has changed drastically. Or even if the management team is keenly aware of the changes, it waits too long before addressing them.

External challenges can be of very different kinds. For instance the automotive industry is facing large challenges:

—— The rise of electric vehicles invalidates their long experience in designing combustion engines, making them vulnerable to new entrants;

—— The younger generations are less interested in owning a car;

—— Autonomous driving, which is becoming an important differentiation feature, favors tech companies that play by a set of completely different rules.

To be able to face deep challenges like these, you need courage. The willingness to succeed must be greater than the knee-jerk reaction of covering your flaws.

But you also need teamwork.

INTENSIFY COLLABORATION

One of the harsh realities you will probably observe on the gemba is that members of the C-level team are defending their own turf at the expense of the others - one of the symptoms of the Big Company Disease. They all have individual objectives, but the system falls apart at the interfaces between them: how product and engineering work together, how sales and marketing interact, etc.

This is a systemic phenomenon, a situation all companies find themselves into if not counterbalanced efficiently by an active effort from the CEO.

Teamwork is a skill: the executive team needs to learn how to work together, led by the CEO. The lean approach relies again on Orient & Support:

— Align all the team on a common, compelling goal

— Help them find out how they can contribute individually, and how they can help their peers succeed

This is a recipe for intensifying collaboration, in order to blur the silos that slow the company down.

But just talking about this is not enough, as verbal communication has its shortcomings, even more in heated group discussions: not everyone talks in the group, we put different meanings on the same words, etc.

The lean approach to collaboration is based on visualization. We make visible what we each have in mind to surface out misunderstandings and misconceptions, and then face them. This is the role of the Obeya, or "large room" in Japanese.

Time to practice

THE OBEYA

What you need for this in practice is a large room where the C-level team can meet every week, in front of large visuals representing the shared meaning they build together.

What is displayed is mostly up to you, but you will find a guide on this page as a starting point. Finding what is important to display and talk about is part of the journey.

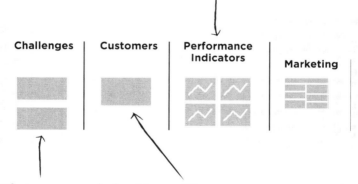

How do we measure our progress? What are the concrete goals we want to achieve?

What are our goals for this year? For the next 5 years? What challenges do we need to face?

What are our customers telling us? What are their own challenges, and how can we help them?

Time to practice

A typical weekly meeting in the obeya involves:

— Studying a customer problem in depth, to focus the team again and again on the end customer

— One member of the team presenting a finished PDCA that shows what was tried and learned to make progress on the collective goal

The mistake you want to avoid is using the Obeya and your weekly meetings as yet another opportunity to create and supervise action plans, in Command & Control mode. The Obeya is a place for exploration, for heated, yet constructive debate, to face the open-ended challenges for which no quick action plan will do. It's a place for learning.

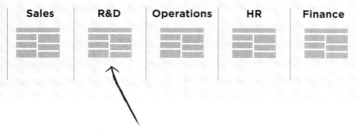

What are we changing in the company's core systems? Do we agree on the changes? How can we help each other in making these changes?

HALVE THE BAD, DOUBLE THE GOOD

How do you choose which metrics to improve and which problems to solve? The lean strategy is based on a set of fundamental challenges which are proven to foster growth:

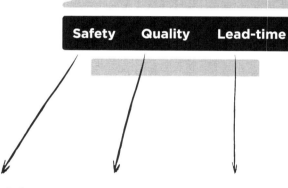

How can we halve the number of physical and psychological accidents?

This can be measured in incident numbers, sick leave days or turnover rate.

How can we halve the number of defects?

Typical measures include volume of incidents, defects or customer reclamations.

How can we halve our lead time?

This is usually measured in terms of average lead time, or in a percentage of deliveries performed on time.

Cost   **Energy Performance**

How can we double our productivity?

Productivity is calculated as the daily number of defect-free items shipped divided by the total number of people.

How can we halve our environmental footprint?

This can be physical waste such as scrap, or energy consumption.

A DIFFERENT OUTLOOK ON FINANCE

You may have noticed that the elements of the lean strategy depicted until now are all based on down to earth operational topics. This does not mean that a lean strategy ignores financial issues - on the contrary, companies that successfully pursue this approach see great financial returns, both in terms of revenue and profit.

The key here is to recognize that finance and operations are two faces of the same coin. The challenges mentioned before translate into concrete financial gains:

- **Quality** has a direct impact on cost, and thus profits, because it's much cheaper to do the job only once. It's also important for customer retention, and thus revenue.

- **Lead-time** reduction lowers the need for cash and helps reduce costs by surfacing inefficiencies. Shorter lead times also benefit the top line, because ultra-fast delivery is a key driver in purchase decisions.

What makes these physical quantities important is that they are leading indicators. You can address them on a day-to-day basis, with all the members of the company, rather than wasting time on line-by-line analysis of financial reports which is akin to driving by looking in the rear mirror.

This leads to a very different kind of financial report: the Plain English P & L.

📢 Time to practice

PLAIN ENGLISH P & L

The Plain English Profit & Loss statement is the main financial tool of the lean CEO. It links financial values with physical, concrete quantities.

As with all visuals, this one should be concise—a single A4 is a good target.

This is an important tool for practicing the helicopter dive: starting from a bird's-eye view of the business, where should you go for your next gemba walk? And what should you look for?

You will find on the left a Plain English P & L for a ride-sharing company, showing what operational metrics could be improved to stimulate the growth of the company in financial terms.

What would be the model for your company?

Time to practice

5 — THE PRACTICE FACE

	Jan	Feb	Mar	...
Revenue				
EBITDA				
Cash				
% employee turnover				
% driver turnover				
% customer churn				
# customer center calls				
Customer waiting time				
Productivity (rides / driver)				
...				

Physical, observable quantities that govern the financial performance metrics

FRAME TO FORM
_____

FRAME

Align the whole company around compelling learning goals

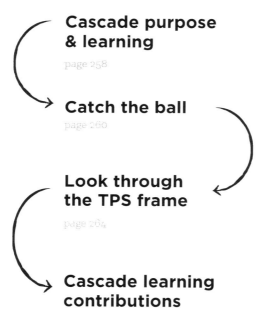

Cascade purpose & learning
page 258

Catch the ball
page 260

Look through the TPS frame
page 264

Cascade learning contributions
page 268

5 — THE PRACTICE — FRAME

5
THE PRACTICE FRAME

CASCADE PURPOSE & LEARNING

You have Faced the main challenges of your business with the executive team, now how do you engage the whole company in addressing them?

In a 4D approach, now would be the time to create a global roadmap with actions for each department and key performance indicators to track progress—but at the risk of feeding the Big Company Disease, each department head protecting its own turf regardless of the overall result.

You can promote teamwork and learning across the organization by steering away from the usual top-down approach and following two main principles.

1. Align teams based on performance and learning challenges, not on actions to execute. This means cascading two questions throughout the organization:

— How can we contribute to the overall objective?

— What do we need to learn, through PDCA experiments, in order to succeed?

2. Build consensus. Alignment is neither purely top-down or bottom-up: it is the result of a global negotiation, everyone contributing to a common goal through a process known as "catch the ball."

5

THE PRACTICE FRAME

CATCH THE BALL

Catch the ball is a discussion, with management looking for voluntary participation in the company's strategy.

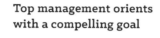

Top management orients with a compelling goal

"This is the global challenge for our company"

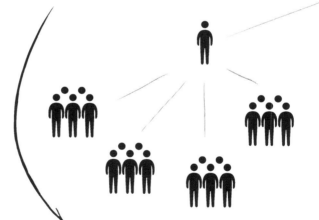

The process involves many one-on-one and group discussions, with department heads setting their own goals and negotiating with the others. In the end, the executive team needs to come up with a coherent strategy to reach the collective goal.

GOALS THAT FOSTER LEARNING

The goals shared by the executive and those set by the departments and teams remain measurable goals, as in any company. The key point here is to use goals as a tool for learning and discovery, instead of a means for pushing an action plan.

Publish 10 job descriptions
on the 5 most visible job boards

Deliver the new global claims
processing workflow

One quarterly team-building event
per department

Command & Control

These goals are meant for enforcing
the execution of known actions

Give a proposal to candidates in less than 5 days after the first contact

Reduce the lead time of claims processing by 50%

Reach an employee satisfaction rating of 4 / 5

Orient & Support

These goals leave open the way to reach them, so that people can find their own solutions

LOOK THROUGH THE TPS FRAME

Setting high level goals is not enough. Teams may get stuck on large goals, failing to see how to attain them. What usually happens is that they try to compensate by just working harder, until they give up and start negotiating the objectives.

Example	Improvement Dimension
Increase the percentage of marketing newsletters accepted right first time by the customer	Quality
Reduce the time needed to setup a crowdfunding campaign	Lead time
Reduce costs in a scooter maintenance service	Cost
Reduce energy consumption of data centers	Environmental impact

The role of management is to frame the goals in such a way that large problems can be explored through a series of daily experiments, close to the reality of the teams.

The TPS is in itself a set of frames designed to do just that.

TPS Frames Examples

Stop the line (andon) at every step in the process to prevent quality issues from reaching customers
Red bins to analyze and remove causes of defects

Takt and Heijunka to coordinate actions
One-piece flow to completely finish a setup before starting another

Takt to align cycle times across the process
Pull to avoid overproduction and surface problems.

Lead-time reduction of application transactions
TPM to increase the availability of servers and reduce the need for redundancy

WHAT ABOUT OKR?

Every company needs a mechanism to align the efforts of individual teams and departments. The Objectives and Key Results (OKR) system, pioneered by companies such as Intel and Google, has gained lots of popularity among tech companies over the years.

	Command & Control
Target	KPIs to evaluate (reward and punish)
How	Solutions to put in place to reach the goal
Motivation	Extrinsic: getting the financial reward by hitting the targets given by the bosses

This system is suited to a Lean Strategy, but what counts is less the tool than the intention. Like all tools, using it as a Command & Control mechanism will expose the business to the Big Company Disease.

Maybe an upgrade would be to call it OKL, for Objectives & Key Learnings?

Orient & Support
Shared compelling goal (looking for energy and alignment)
Exploration topics to drive learning and reach the goal
Intrinsic: creating value and making progress as a team with a sense of purpose

🔊 **Time to practice**

CASCADING LEARNING CONTRIBUTIONS

As an alignment practice, there are two levels to address: company-wide, and at the department or team level. Answering the questions below will help you clarify the goals at each level.

Framing the Collective Goal

How do you create value and for whom?	
What makes your company different?	
What is the compelling goal you want to achieve in the next 5 years? At the end of this year?	

Framing Team Contributions

How do you contribute to the overall goal?	
What is the improvement dimension you work upon, in the TPS frame?	
How will you measure progress?	
What is the target performance?	

FORM TO FIND

FORM

Innovate every day to stay relevant over time

Develop creative thinking through kaizen
page 274

Propagate reusable learning
page 278

Cadence product evolutions
page 286

Quality / Function deployment
page 292

5 — THE PRACTICE — FORM

5

THE PRACTICE

FORM

DEVELOP CREATIVE THINKING THROUGH KAIZEN

Having Framed the challenges of the company into concrete, day-to-day improvement ideas, the teams can now Form new solutions to specific problems in a flow of quick, daily experiments.

For instance, « improving the quality of our marketing campaigns » results, for a given team member, on Tuesday morning, in clarifying the quality expectations of a new Christmas campaign for a specific customer. What does quality mean in this specific context? What can she try to make it work correctly the first time? How will she measure the results? And how will she share what she learned? At this point, she is Forming a specific solution to the problem in this specific context.

You are not looking for a global solution. You are learning how to approach a global challenge in many different contexts.

Forming solutions is not always a matter of traditional problem-solving, trying to figure out the root cause of an abnormal situation. The normal situation may not be enough anymore.

Once the situation is under control, what is needed to increase performance is creativity. This is the ultimate goal of the lean strategy: creating the conditions for everyone to bring their initiative and their creativity at work every day to create more value for customers.

This is the purpose of kaizen.

5

THE PRACTICE

FORM

Time to practice

6-STEP KAIZEN

One of the roles of the team leader is to lead an activity of continuous improvement in his team.
Selecting the improvement topic is key. You want it to be:

- Motivating for the team
- Relevant to their day-to-day activity
- A small step forward, reachable in a matter of days or weeks, not months

Typical kaizen topics include:
- Reducing the response time of a software application
- Fixing underperforming marketing campaigns
- Reducing the editing time of videos, etc.

Managing the improvement effort still follows the PDCA logic, but with a different twist. The problem solving approach presented earlier is all about digging into root causes to understand why an activity is getting out of standard. Kaizen, on the other hand, is about developing the team's creativity to imagine and test novel ideas, looking for a better standard.

When you visit a team, you expect to see their kaizen displayed on the wall, following the six steps shown on the right. Clarity is key: you want to understand the situation at a glance.

Time to practice

1 **Define improvement potential**	Is the gain clear for the team? Are they passionate about it? Look for a small step, attainable fairly quickly. You want to avoid embarking on a PhD.
2 **Analyze current methods**	What is the main blocking point—the point where creativity is really needed? This should result from a detailed analysis of current work practices.
3 **Generate original ideas**	What are really new approaches to this problem? What are the best doing elsewhere? Which ideas do we want to try?
4 **Develop an implementation plan**	How can we try the new ideas as quickly as possible? How will we evaluate the results?
5 **Implement the plan**	Who do we need to notify? How can we proceed fast, in a positive atmosphere?
6 **Evaluate the new method**	What works and what doesn't? How do we avoid falling back to the old ways?

PROPAGATE REUSABLE LEARNING

As the teams perform kaizen and come up with innovative ideas, it is tempting to deploy the newly found solutions throughout the company. There are two risks here: imposing solutions that will not fit the target context, and developing the Big Company Disease by feeding people with ready-to-use solutions instead of developing their own initiative.

How can you propagate knowledge in this case?

A first step consists of keeping the knowledge in work standards that capture only the key points of what was learned. But the deeper answer is to think in terms of reusable learning instead of reusable knowledge.

Reusable learning is about sharing not only the result, but the complete PDCA story of how the team went about solving a problem. This lets other teams benefit from the acquired knowledge while preserving the ability to think and experiment on their own.

The last phase of the six-step kaizen cycle involves the team presenting their approach and their findings to all the teams that could benefit from that knowledge.

This is how the company develops new capabilities over time. Challenges are turned into new types of kaizen, which are propagated across the company so that teams learn how to approach them.

Learning, however, is not just limited to the capabilities of people. It feeds the new generations of products.

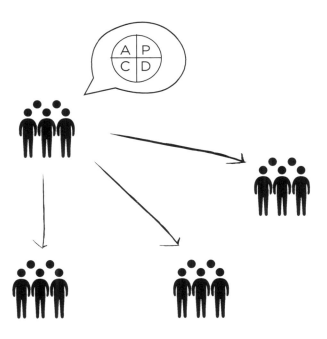

IMPROVING PRODUCTS

By solving problems across the company every day, with a strong focus on satisfying customer needs, you gain valuable insights into the limits of the current generation of products, with major opportunities for improvement everywhere. You can better see:

- **What customers are trying to achieve, (i.e. the problem they are trying to solve)**
- **What they look for in the current product**
- **How the current product fails them**
- **Why they switch to other products or from other products**
- **How team members struggle with internal tools**
- **How team members could work better with the right tools**

In a typical company, you would log new feature requests for the product development team and the engineering department. These features would then join a large list of other features, waiting to be prioritized—probably for months—before being implemented.

To get out of this situation and develop the right products fast, you need to take a step back and reconsider how products are built.

5

THE PRACTICE

FORM

THE LIMITS OF ADDING FEATURES

Many people in the company are submitting product evolution ideas, without any expertise in how to build a good product. They usually propose evolutions in the form of solutions, without any clear problem to be solved.

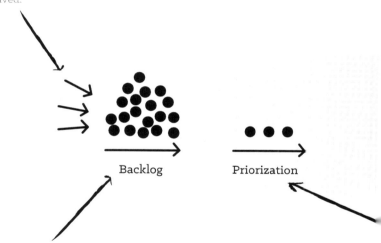

The road map is always full of ideas to test, which leads to the following consequences:
- Products become inevitably bloated
- Adding feature upon feature makes it difficult for engineers to maintain high levels of quality
- Profits are squandered on nice-to-have product evolutions, making the company more vulnerable.

With the advent of agile software development approaches, the current model of engineering organizations is that of the "feature production machine".

While it is key to be able to implement a flow of small evolutions and get quick feedback from users, adopting this approach as a main product strategy has its drawbacks. The usual symptoms are the following:

Developers lack the information and support needed from other departments (marketing, sales, operations, etc.). They often realize that features are incoherent or serve no real needs, but they have little leverage on how features are chosen.

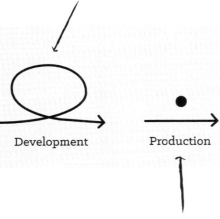

Development   Production

The product evolves as a result of a negotiation between executives. This "design by committee" leads to products that lack focus.

The core product is shipped, but the remaining activities (user support, training, documentation) is given lip service. As a consequence, the business results of the evolution - if any - are only partially obtained.

A CHIEF ENGINEER TO INTENSIFY TEAMWORK

The Lean Strategy relies on a specific approach to building products, based on a simple idea: good thinking, good products.

To build a great product, the needs and constraints from all the dimensions of the company—customers, operations, marketing sales, etc.—must be integrated into a coherent whole. This requires an intense collaboration between representatives from many different departments, but how do you achieve it?

The key lies in the role of the chief engineer. The chief engineer is the CEO of the product, responsible for delivering business results at a given date and within a given cost target. As someone with deep experience and a real passion for the product, the chief engineer is no mere project manager. She owns the product decisions, not just the planning.

The chief engineer:

- Creates a vision of customer preferences
- Defines and gets agreement from all executives on a product concept
- Strives to improve the product for the customer perspective while keeping changes as focused and minimal as possible

— Manages an intense collaboration between functions to resolve the many problems that arise during product development

Depending on the context, the chief engineer is either the chief product officer, a product manager, a product owner, the CEO, the CTO, etc. Whatever the official title, the chief engineer is anyone who:

— Takes ultimate responsibility for the design and delivery of the product
— Dedicates herself entirely to client satisfaction
— Has a passion for the product, including the competitors' products
— Is willing to get involved in technical and functional problems
— Has the full support of top management

Where does the chief engineer start? Keeping everyone synchronized to deliver on time is again a question of Just-in-Time, so this person starts with defining a Takt of product evolutions.

CADENCE PRODUCT EVOLUTIONS

A product does not usually live in isolation: it follows previous generations of products, and is replaced by a newer generation. This is even the case for seemingly new products: for instance the computer-assisted word editor followed the typewriter, which followed handwriting. Products follow one another in a flow, solving customer problems which keep evolving over time.

Product Takt

Value Engineering **Value Analysis** /

Study existing products in production
to better understand user needs,
and see where the current technology
is failing

Identify the key product characteristics
which need to be improved to bring
the expected business results

The chief engineer evolves the product generation after generation, following a given Takt - much like Apple's iPhones line which gives birth to a new version every year.

Every generation is built following the value analysis / value engineering cycle:

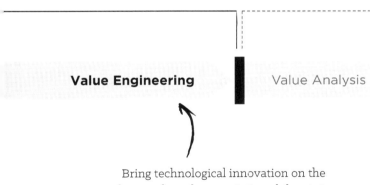

Bring technological innovation on the key product characteristics while minimizing the changes on the product and the company operations

◀||▶ **Time to practice**

PRODUCT EVOLUTIONS TAKT

Having a fixed, repeating cadence of updates for every product in your portfolio is key to:

— Aligning everyone in the company on a shared cadence
— Balancing resources between products
— Making sure that all products remain relevant, since you don't wait for them to be obsolete before reacting
— Keeping customers interested with a familiar rhythm of product news

You can use the table on the right to visualize the takt time for each product. At what pace do customers expect changes for each one?

Note that this applies not only to physical or digital products; it is also relevant for services.

Time to practice

	Q1	Q2	Q3	Q4	Q1	Q2	Q3	Q4
Product 1	/		/		/		/	
Product 2		/				/		
Product 3				/				/

FROM FEATURES TO PRODUCT CHARACTERISTICS

Product evolutions from one version of the product to the next are not just features to be added, but challenges that require learning.

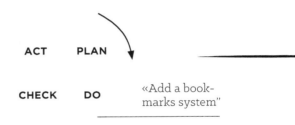

ACT	PLAN
CHECK	DO

«Add a bookmarks system"

Command & Control

The product or engineering team is given a solution to execute, with two risks:

— They could have come up with a more effective or less expensive solution
— With a focus on execution, there is very little chance that the business results will be checked - and obtained

As with the cascading goals of the Frame phase, this requires a different way to think about goals:

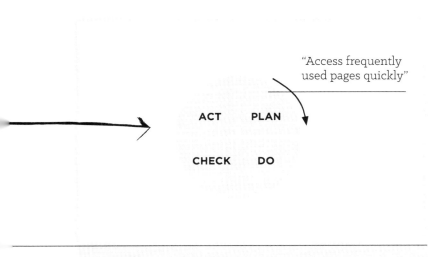

Orient & Support

The product or engineering team is given a challenge: find a technical solution to improve a key characteristic of the product.

It can then use the PDCA cycle to check different solutions and learn.

⏸ Time to practice

QUALITY/ FUNCTION DEPLOYMENT

To think deeper about the next version of your product, you can use a simplified Quality / Function Deployment (QFD) matrix as shown on the right.

This table shows how quality (customer expectations) is deployed on functions (technical solutions, features or technologies), in the case of a mail client application.
Designing products customers want to buy is a rich and multifaceted discipline, worth an entire book on its own. Answering the two main questions of the QFD matrix will put you on the right path to creating better products.

What are the customer preferences or product characteristics for your target segment?

Time to practice

What resources, solutions, or technologies do you put in place to improve these characteristics?

	Background updates	Priority view		
Loads fast	●			
Do not miss new emails		●		
Do not forget responding to emails				
Can work offline				

5

THE PRACTICE | FORM

THE LEAN
STRATEGY

———————

THE ANTIDOTE

The Big Company Disease is inescapable - it will keep creeping inevitably as the company grows. The 4F cycle provides you with the means to slow it down:

Defending **process** over **customers**

Defending **silos** over **teamwork**

Rewarding **compliance** over **initiative**

Confusing **legacy** and **heritage** technologies

Going to the gemba and pushing the company in a never-ending quest of lead-time reduction with kanban is the opportunity to put the customer again and again at the center of the conversation.

Kanban and the pull system create a counteracting force, pushing everyone to better collaborate across value streams. In addition, working with the C-level team in the Obeya, you can fight the silos at their core: the relations between executives.

With a structure of team leaders trained to support team members, you can develop a kaizen spirit across the organization: the daily pursuit of creative ideas to deliver more value to customers and society.

Studying customer complaints and facing the problems faced every day by the teams helps everybody better understand what must be kept and what must change.

But fighting the Big Company Disease is not an end in itself. It is necessary for the company to adapt and grow.

THE PRODUCT/ MARKET FIT MACHINE

Ultimately, the lean strategy is a strategy of constant adaptation to market conditions.

Every 4F cycle is the opportunity to sense changes in the market, and then to explore new ways to adapt. And at the same time, every 4F cycle develops the capability of the whole organization to better sense what is going on outside, and to better collaborate to react to these changes.

What makes the lean strategy unique is that it provides an operational model for an always adapting company, with a specific approach. Starting from the evolution of the company and its context, it constantly reframes the reflection around the ultimate lean question :

Who needs to learn what in order for the company to succeed?

This leaves us with one last, and fundamental, exercise.

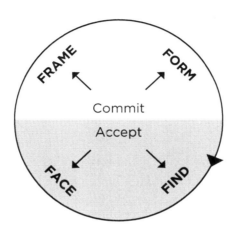

Time to practice

PLAN PER PERSON

In the end, the adaptability of the company boils down to that of each individual. The main lean question is: Who needs to learn what in order for the company to succeed? This is not a rhetorical question. It is a very concrete exercise to be performed by the executive team on a regular basis.

You can start considering every person in your team, department or company, trying to clarify the next challenge that will help her grow.

Who	Autonomous in
Susan	Producing and improving landing pages, newsletters and search advertising campaigns

Time to practice

Next development area	Challenge
Building and coordinating complete multi-channel marketing campaigns with her colleagues	Christmas campaign: Improve online sales by 20% over last year while keeping the same acquisition costs

CONCLUSION

As the world enters a period of profound change, there are many exciting opportunities ahead:

—— Young talent wants to join companies where they feel listened to. They want to learn and grow quickly, and they want to serve a good cause.

—— Customers are looking for richer relationships with companies able to provide them with custom-tailored, yet affordable products and services.

—— Society at large is expecting the corporate world to be less wasteful of natural resources, but without giving up on the comfort that we have all grown accustomed to.

We believe that the Lean Strategy is the best approach to seize these opportunities. It is perfectly suited to modern expectations, yet proven over decades by hundreds of companies. It is the right blend of competition and care. It is built for adaptation and resilience. And it is not just concepts and theories: the lean practice is well known and grounded in reality.

CEOs and managers of modern tech companies are proving that this model works, and gives them an edge in scaling up their companies while retaining the ability to adjust to ever-changing conditions.

You can be a part of this too. What it takes is just to get out of your office to go and see, ask "Why?" Then show respect.

TIME TO PRACTICE!

FIND

Engage people in improving the company by solving operational problems day in and day out, while developing their skills and their ability to work together. This series of exercises needs to be repeated for each value stream in your company :
—— Customer support
—— Operations
—— Product development
—— Recruitment
—— Finance
—— etc.

page

- [ ] Start a **gemba walk routine** by dedicating specific slots in your calendar — page 106

- [ ] Set up a **customer board** to better understand how to retain customers — page 122

- [ ] Set up a **kanban** to make your lead time visual and uncover problems — page 148

- [ ] Start a **daily problem solving** activity — page 154

- ○ Identify your team leaders and establish an **andon** system *page 196*

- ○ Help team members take ownership of their workplace with a **5S** program *page 218*

- ○ Involve teams in creating **standards** to distinguish normal from abnormal situations. *page 232*

- ○ Perform **red bins** analysis with your teams to improve quality at every step *page 206*

- ○ Perform a **variability analysis** to dig into the causes of delays *page 168*

- ○ Pursue **continuous one-piece flow** to drive improvement *page 184*

- ○ Visualize your **product mix** to clarify activities and value streams *page 172*

- ○ Compute the **takt time** to better balance work across teams *page 178*

- ○ Create a **leveled production plan** (heijunka) to create stability *page 224*

- ○ Set up a **pull system** to improve teamwork across the company *page 188*

FACE

Uncover the main factors that limit the growth of your company. Face your own responsibility, and bring the executive team to agree on tackling these challenges together.

    page

○ Set up an **Obeya** to align your executive team on the main challenges to tackle   page 246

○ Create and maintain a **Plain English P&L** to align your financial and operational challenges   page 252

FRAME

Align the whole company on a small set of operational challenges

    page

○ **Cascade learning contributions** from your C-level to all teams   page 268

FORM

Foster the creativity of everyone in the company to develop new capabilities and adapt to market changes

                                                                  page

- ◯ Start local **kaizen** initiatives to engage your teams in finding better ways to work   page 276

- ◯ Define your **product evolutions takt** to keep your products relevant over time   page 288

- ◯ Create a **quality/function deployment** table to deliver more value for customers   page 292

- ◯ Create and maintain a **plan per person** with all your management team   page 300

6 | THE LEAN STRATEGY

ACKNOWLEDGEMENTS

Ideas are seldom really new, and it is even more true with this book. My main goal here has been to introduce more people to the seminal work of Michael Ballé, Dan Jones, Jacques Chaize and Orest Fiume in The Lean Strategy. Working with Michael Ballé on real-world cases never ceases to reveal deep insights into the richness of lean and business in general. Thanks Michael.

This book is also the result of many gemba walks with the CEOs and practitioners I have had the privilege to work with. Benoît Charles-Lavauzelle was the first in the French Tech ecosystem to understand the potential of lean as a business strategy. Alexandre Mulliez and Jonathan Vidor quickly joined in, and over the years other CEOS and hundreds of people have come in to explore this approach in many different situations. The list is huge, but I am especially indebted to Steve Anavi, Maxime Barbier, Fabrice Bernhard, Aymerik Bouchacourt, Benjamin Cardoso, Nicolas Chartier, Rodolphe Darves-Bornoz, Pierre Derome, Benjamin Grandfond, Julien Jacob, Béryl de Labouchère, Julien Laure, Jérôme Lecat, Laure Lefevre, Thibaud Lemonnier, Sébastien Lucas, Julien Masson, Christophe Riboulet, Woody Rousseau, Guillaume Rouvière and David Sobel. Many thanks also to my colleagues at Keenly and Institut Lean France: Christophe Ordano, Sandrine

Olivencia, Catherine Chabiron, Marc-Antoine Lacroix and Pierre Palliez.

Finding the right approach and completing the manuscript was a job I could not do alone. Thanks to Marie-Hortense Varin, Caroline Sauvegrain, Emmanuelle Bach-Donnard and Philippe Fenot for their precious feedback. Thanks also to Barbara Sapik and Hanna Pfestorf for their fantastic work on the book design.

Finally, I would like to thank my family, Séverine, Chloé, Romeo and Tom, who had to put up with me getting glued on my computer during numerous week-ends and what was supposed to be a family holiday at the beach.

JOIN THE COMMUNITY

You can get more information and join our community here:

https://learningtoscale.co

6

THE LEAN STRATEGY

Legal deposit : April 2020

Printed in Poland
by Amazon Fulfillment
Poland Sp. z o.o., Wrocław